How to Have a
Fabulous
Life—
No Matter *What*
Comes Your Way

Other Books by Karen Linamen

Chocolatherapy: Satisfying the Deepest Cravings of Your Inner Chick

I'm Not Suffering from Insanity, I'm Enjoying Every Minute of It

Welcome to the Funny Farm

Sometimes I Wake Up Grumpy (and Sometimes I Let Him Sleep)

Just Hand Over the Chocolate and No One Will Get Hurt

Pillow Talk: The Intimate Marriage from A to Z

And for Children

Princess Madison and the Royal Darling Pageant

Princess Madison and the Whispering Woods

Princess Madison and the Paisley Puppy

How to Have a
Fabulous Life—
No Matter *What* Comes Your Way

Karen Scalf Linamen

SPIRE

© 2008 by Karen Scalf Linamen

Published by Revell
a division of Baker Publishing Group
P.O. Box 6287, Grand Rapids, MI 49516-6287
www.revellbooks.com

Spire edition published 2009

ISBN 978-0-8007-8795-0

Previously published under the title *Due to Rising Energy Costs, the Light at the End of the Tunnel Has Been Turned Off*

Printed in the United States of America

09 10 11 12 13 14 15   7 6 5 4 3 2 1

Peace. It does not mean to be in a place where there is no noise, trouble or hard work. It means to be in the midst of those things and still be calm in your heart.

Author unknown

All things splendid have been achieved by those who dared believe that something inside of them was superior to circumstance.

Bruce Barton

Contents

Introduction

I don't know about you, but what goes on in my world gets under my skin.

I wish I could feel peaceful, happy, and vibrant all the time, but the truth is that stuff bothers me. Big stuff, little stuff, it doesn't matter. It all has the potential to trip me up and send me reeling.

In other words, when things in my life—like relationships, career, finances, my environment, and even my body—aren't going as planned (and when it comes to my body, things *never* seem to go as planned!), my emotions follow. Kind of like faithful puppies panting after their master—or like lambs to the slaughter.

All it takes is a dozen bounced checks in a month (don't laugh; it's happened) or a health crisis or an unexpected bill or a critical word from a friend, and my spirits can take a nosedive. A week of sleepless nights with a new baby, an argument with a husband, or the fact that the sewer line backed up in the basement *again* can do the same thing. And let's not even talk about what happens to our emotions over a softening jawline or twenty extra pounds. Suddenly we're anything but peaceful. Yesterday we might have been on cloud nine, but today we're down in the dumps. Instead of feeling alive, confident, and excited about the future, we feel exhausted, bored, trapped, or depressed.

What if you and I could free our emotions from the tyranny of our circumstances, if we could loosen just a little the tether between our spirits and the stuff that goes wrong in our lives? Wouldn't it be great if the next time we found ourselves in unpleasant or even scary circumstances, we knew how to hang on to peace, joy, and hope *anyway*?

Maybe being able to free our emotions from the tyranny of circumstances has something to do with internalizing some of that peace, happiness, and hope, tucking them deep inside so that they're protected and not just hanging out there exposed to all the wind and rain and storms of life.

Or maybe peace, happiness, and hope are like muscles we can learn to flex on our own, even when our circumstances are less than inspiring.

Perhaps it's about attaching our emotions to things *other* than our circumstances, things that are not only kinder and gentler but more stable as well.

Or maybe it's about finding and strengthening our inner core. Just as the inner ear enables us to stay balanced whether we're sitting, standing, bending over, or riding in an elevator, you and I need a strong inner core that can keep us stable and moving forward when circumstances threaten to send us spiraling.

Can we *really* experience a happy, even fabulous life no matter what the world throws our way?

The answer, my friend, is yes. And together we're going to figure out how.

1

The Light at the End of the Tunnel
Has Been Turned Off

Nobody likes frustration or shame or depression or panic or gloom, especially when there are so many other emotions to choose from!

For example, there's everybody's favorite. Of course I'm talking about that "falling in love" feeling and it's giddifying, isn't it? Sure, it's all-consuming and tends to eclipse everything else in our lives, like being productive at work and remembering to pay the water bill on time, but other than that, who wouldn't love to feel that way every day?

Then there's that victorious feeling, like when you grab the last pair of leopard-print pumps on the clearance rack at Macy's—and they happen to be your size.

Or how 'bout the "Ohmigosh I can't believe this is happening to me!" feeling you get when you win the lottery or hear your name announced as the winner of the Miss America Pageant? (Not that I actually know what that feels like, but I imagine it's got to feel pretty good!)

On the other hand, there's the feeling you get when the police siren starts wailing behind you, and, looking down at your speedometer, you wince because it's still registering twenty-two miles over the limit, even though you took your foot off the accelerator as soon as you spotted Deputy Fife parked on the side of the highway pointing a hair dryer in your direction. On second thought, let's not put this one on the list.

There are certainly a lot of emotion options. Practically speaking, though, here are three of my favorites, feelings I'd love to experience every single day: I'd love to stay in touch with a sense of inner calm, a good dose of happiness, and that feeling that good things are coming my way.

Peace, joy, and hope. If you ask me, it's a trio that's even better than cookies and milk and . . . well . . . more cookies.

Who turned out the lights?

So what's stopping us? Why aren't you and I happy, peaceful, and vibrant with hope every single day of our lives? Oh *yeah*. I remember why.

Stuff. All the stuff that happens all around us all the time: relationship stuff, career stuff, money stuff; making a home, making a living, and making do with unmet needs in any category; broken dreams, big boo-boos, little letdowns; memories that hurt, shoes that pinch, bosses that pinch. The Pinscher next door that ate your cat.

Or maybe it's swimsuits that shrink two sizes over the winter, shrinking eyebrows, that ring around your toilet bowl, that ringing in your ears, and the wedding ring on the finger of the cute guy you just met in the peanut butter aisle of your local Piggly Wiggly. It could be that bad news phone call, the creep who broke your daughter's heart, the promotion that went to the assistant you hired on the same day your fortune cookie said, "It doesn't look good. Maybe you should have stayed in bed."

Nine months ago I had a significant relationship stop on a dime and propel me into a good five months of depression. When I think back on memories from those months, the images that come to mind are really dark. And I mean literally. I remember charcoal storm clouds gathering over the forest outside my bedroom window, chilly twilights morphing into starless evenings, shadows in my room in the middle of the day.

What strikes me now is that the relationship ended in June.

June!

Where I live, June is the month with the sunniest mornings, longest days, and brightest skies. And yet most of my memories from that time are framed in shadows.

So why aren't you and I glowing with all the happiness, inner calm, and hope that we desire and adore?

Because pretty much every day of our lives, something somewhere is happening in our individual world that—if we let it—can dim those good feelings. In fact sometimes our circumstances can *really* trip us up, sending us plunging into complete emotional darkness and even despair.

Looking for peace, joy, and hope in all the wrong places

There's no denying that our circumstances produce the seeds of joy, pain, triumph, sorrow, and more. And actually it's a *good* thing that the stuff in our lives gets on our nerves and under our skin. This is because people who remain completely unmoved by anything life sends their way are not only experiencing a psychotic break with reality, but should probably think twice before standing in front of an oncoming truck.

I think where I go wrong isn't that I let my circumstances *influence* my emotional well-being; too often I let them *determine* my emotional well-being. In other words, I'm convinced we get into trouble when we get in the habit of drawing our peace, joy, hope, as well as our purpose, direction, and motivation from our circumstances *and nothing else*.

I like to think of peace, joy, and hope as internal forces, kinda like muscles. After all, they give us strength. They can determine our path, get us moving, and keep us on track. They help us embrace and even change our world. My friend Candy raises three kids, one neurotic friend (me), and a couple of horses—all from a wheelchair due to a boating accident twelve years ago. I asked her which she would rather live without—the full use of her legs or emotions like peace and joy and hope. Her answer?

Do you have this yet?

So if peace, joy, and hope are internal forces—emotional muscles and vital ones at that—why in the world would we relinquish power over these vital muscles to *external* forces, some of which we can control but many of which we can't? After all, we wouldn't give complete and utter control of our physical muscles to outside influences, like, say, Hollywood celebrities, would we? What if we could use our legs only when Brad and Angie adopted another baby? What would happen if we could flex our fingers only on days Britney Spears made Yahoo headlines, or we could turn our head only when Johnny Depp released a new *Pirates* flick?

The image that comes to mind is that of a marionette. I can't speak for anyone else, but *I* don't want my limbs jerked around by anyone who's made the cover of the *Weekly World News*. So why should I let my emotional muscles get jerked around by external circumstances over which I have limited or no control?

Everything I need to know about life I learned in belly dancing class

I take belly dancing lessons. Not that I'm any good—I've taken classes with four different teachers in three states and have spent several hundred dollars on hip scarves, and I *still* look like C3PO in *Star Wars* when I dance.

Still . . .

There's something amazing about the dance. One thing that fascinates me is the fact that the moves are so isolated. Take the head slide, for example. You've seen it, I'm sure. It's the Cleopatra-looking move where you keep your head completely vertical and move it from side to side. Try it without moving your shoulders.

Or what about the move where you move your hips from side to side in a completely horizontal line without moving the upper part of your body, not even a teensy bit.

I love all the isolations. They take a lot of concentration, forcing you to identify and work separate muscle groups. I still practice them one at a time, although I am trying to learn how to do two at once. A *real* dancer can layer many at the same time. And even though her dancing looks fluid and whole, I know enough about the art to realize that it looks that way because she has invested time learning how to perform each move without disrupting the beauty of the others. In other words, her hip slide looks just as graceful whether it's being performed alone or she surrounds it with a flurry of footwork, shoulder shimmies, and body rolls.

That's how I want my emotional muscles to work.

I want to exercise peace until it comes just as naturally all by itself or surrounded by a flurry of circumstances that may or may not be peaceful.

I want to exercise joy until it comes just as naturally all by itself or surrounded by a flurry of circumstances that may or may not generate happiness.

And I want to exercise hope until it comes just as naturally alone or surrounded by a flurry of circumstances that may or may not encourage hope.

Oh, I almost forgot.

You remember how I mentioned all the stuff muscles do? I said they give us strength, determine our path, get us going, keep us on track, and even help us change our world.

There's something else they do for us.

When we find ourselves flat on our face in a dark place, muscles get us back on our feet, moving toward an exit, and reaching for the switch that makes the world shiny and bright once again. And the next time the light goes out at the end of one of your tunnels, a well-toned sense of peace, hope, and joy can do the very same thing.

In the following chapters, we're going to talk about twelve ways we can stretch, flex, and tone our peace, joy, and hope—every day, rain or shine, even when it's dark outside, *especially* when it's dark outside.

Life is too short and too rich for anything less. After all, you and I've got places to go, things to do, people to love, life to live, and dances to dance. Who wants to stay home in bed because of a little inclement weather?

The bad news is that sometimes skies are gray.

The good news is that you and I don't run on solar power.

Whether we realize it or not, we really do have the moxie we need to tone the emotional muscles that will help us get the most mileage and joy out of our lives. Even if we *do* look like C3PO when we belly dance.

Turn on a Light

- How much do your day-to-day circumstances influence your emotions?

- Does it take something major to send your emotions reeling or can trivial things have the same result?

- Is the idea that you can free your emotions from the tyranny of your circumstances a new concept for you or is this something you've always known was possible?

- In the past what have you done to raise your spirits above whatever circumstances were bringing you down? Were you successful?

- Between peace, joy, and hope, is there one feeling in particular that seems to be missing in your life? Which one?

2

The Face Is Familiar but I Can't Quite Remember the Name

My sister Renee, her husband Harald, and their three boys just moved into town, and I couldn't be more thrilled.

I am going to have to look into nametags, however. It was embarrassing enough when several years ago I started addressing my younger daughter, Kacie, by saying things like, "KaitlynImeanKacie, is your room clean?"

As my older daughter, Kaitlyn, hit her teens, something about her perky smile and long dark hair must have reminded me of my own sister at that age, because before long I found myself addressing her as "Kacie-ImeanReneeImeanKaitlyn."

Sometimes I must be really out of it because on more than one occasion the name Walter has crept into the mix. Walter is the white German shepherd we used to have.

It's dawning on me that those were the good ol' days, because now things are *completely* out of control. This is because, with both my sisters living close—and all of our kids practically inseparable—I can frequently be heard spouting some form of the following: "Hunter-ImeanConnorImeanGabriellaImeanIsaacImeanKaitlyn ImeanKacie . . ." Sometimes I resort to the generic, "You . . . yeah *you* . . . the one with the blond hair . . ."

I don't know what's up with my fading memory (and don't bother to email me, "It's because you're getting old," because I'll just forget you ever said that).

All I know is that sometimes things don't stick around in my brain like I want them to.

Do elephants ever need therapy?

At the same time, some memories are more stubborn than cellulite. No matter how many years come and go, these images seem as vivid and real as the day they were burned into my brain. And more times than not, they're memories of the hurts, disappointments, and failures that have provided my various therapists with gainful employment for decades.

Maybe our brains are a little like wallets filled with photos. Except, unlike snapshots of toothless first graders and teens in prom gowns and tuxedos, some of these photos can be pretty gruesome, not unlike glossies of crime scenes and autopsies.

My guess is that you know exactly what I'm talking about. You've got the same kind of images in your brain

22

too, don't you? These are the memories that keep us awake all night, biting our lower lips and feeling anxious. They fill us with fear or make us writhe with guilt or regret or keep us pining away for something we lost or a second chance we'll never get.

But I think there's something even *worse* that can happen, and it happens when memories of hurts, disappointments, and failures become fodder for our inner Eeyore. In the true spirit of Winnie the Pooh's pessimistic donkey pal, our inner Eeyore is always telling us stuff like, "You probably can't do it this time, either," or "Oh great, another heartbreak waiting to happen," or "Oh look, you messed up. *Again*." Because sometimes, the thing that keeps us awake all night . . . or fills us with fear . . . or makes us writhe with guilt or regret . . . or keeps us pining for things lost . . . isn't the fact that our memories keep handing us vivid images but that our memories are the unseen force shaping our inner dialogue. We're not *picturing* ourselves as a seventh grade wallflower when we tell ourselves—at twenty-seven—that we're a rejection magnet, but that doesn't mean that a painful memory from junior high (and others like it) isn't the ventriloquist behind the voice.

Trust me when I tell you that these two things—hindering memories and a gloomy inner voice—can really keep us from experiencing peace, joy, and hope. In fact they can keep us from feeling secure, happy, and vibrant even when circumstances are great! Haven't you met people who could find something depressing to say about winning the lottery? ("Think of the taxes you'll have to pay.") Or falling in love? ("Enjoy it while it lasts.

He'll be gone tomorrow.") Or a sunny day? ("Hello, melanoma.")

But when circumstances go awry, watch out. Those limiting memories and gloomy inner voice can *really* have a field day.

This is why—if you and I want to have *any* shot at all of experiencing peace, joy, and hope in our day-to-day life—managing our memories is critical.

The stuff memories are made of

We put a lot of stock in memories. They influence us so much that I decided to do some research and find out a little more about memories, like how they're made.

I used to think that, when it came to recording the events in our lives, brains worked kind of like digital cameras. Click, shutter, snap, and images were captured in a way that was objective, accurate, and permanent. But researchers are realizing that our memories aren't created as much by what happened as by what we *think* happened.

Pat Murphy and Paul Doherty have written a fascinating article titled "Messing with Your Mind" in which they describe experiments where vivid memories have been altered—and sometimes even created out of thin air—by really simple factors.[1]

For example, we know now that *things that happen before an event* can impact how we remember that event. Murphy and Doherty give a real-life example of a woman who identified a man in a police lineup because she had a vivid memory of him as the guy who had attacked her. But the man had an airtight alibi. During the attack he had been a guest on a live TV show. So why did she remember him so clearly as her assailant? Turns out she had been watching that very TV show just prior to her attack. Her brain had combined the two separate events—seeing this man's face on TV and, later, being attacked—to form a single vivid, though inaccurate, memory of the assault.

Sometimes *unrelated emotions during an event* can determine the way we remember that event. Remember back in chapter 1 when I talked about my memories of last summer? June in Colorado is filled with bright, long days and plenty of sunshine. And yet, because I was feeling sad and depressed, I have vivid memories of that entire summer being overcast and gray.

On top of all that, *what happens after an event* can change our memory of the event. After two groups viewed a video of a car accident, the group that was asked "How fast were the cars going when they hit?" estimated lower speeds than the group that was asked "How fast were the cars going when they smashed?" To make matters even more interesting, six months later members of the group that was given the question with the word *smashed* were far more likely to remember seeing broken glass in the video, even though there was none. In other words, the folks who were fed the word *smashed* after watching the video altered their memories to accommodate that single word.

Finally, it's easier than you think to have—floating around in your head—*completely imaginary memories.*

Not skewed or altered but detailed memories of stuff that never occurred. Murphy and Doherty give a lot of examples, including one of a young man who was given brief descriptions of five events that were supposed to have happened to him when he was a kid (one of these events—getting lost in the mall—never happened). He was then asked to write a paragraph about each event, filling in details like what he was wearing and so on. When he ranked these five memories in terms of clarity, the imaginary mall incident turned out to be his second most vivid memory of the bunch.

In other words, events don't make our memories. What we *believe* about events—real events and imaginary ones too—makes our memories.

Interesting stuff, huh? But what do we do with it all? On a practical level, how can this help you and me tame our more troublesome memories, especially considering there's a good chance they're not all that trustworthy *anyway*, so that they stop stealing our peace, happiness, and hope?

Hair today, gone tomorrow

Our hairstylist is moving. I say "our" because my mom was the one who discovered Scott Mora, owner of the Genesis Salon here in the Springs, and then got me hooked. In addition to offering a more traditional approach than the feng shui hair experience I wrote about in my previous book, Scott happens to be a hair genius. I get compliments on my hair all the time. Last week my sister Renee eyed my highlights and said, "Hey, can I have that color when you're done with it?"

Mom and I love Scott. He's amazing. He makes us look beautiful. He's moving his shop across town, but that's okay because we'll follow him to the ends of the earth. Okay, *I'll* follow him to the ends of the earth. Mom'll go only as far as the elevator.

She's a little concerned about it. To get to Scott's new shop, she's going to have to park in a parking garage and take an elevator to the second floor. This is a problem because, for the past twenty years, she's been deathly afraid of both elevators and parking garages. They make her panic. Her heart races, her breathing becomes fast and shallow, and she's paralyzed by fear. I mean, Scott's good, but there are limits to how far a girl will go for even a *really* good cut and color.

So about an hour ago over coffee, I was telling Mom about this very chapter and how our memories are influenced by what went on before, during, and even after the experience we *think* we're remembering.

She said, "Funny you should bring this up right now, because something dawned on me just last night. I was fretting over the whole thing with Scott because, well, who wants to lose the best stylist in the universe over an elevator? So I was trying to remember when I started getting these panic attacks and why." And then she told me the story of her very first panic attack.

It was the summer of 1982 and Mom had an appointment with her dentist to take care of an abscessed tooth that had been hurting for weeks. After driving nearly an hour in California rush hour traffic, she arrived at

27

the medical complex flustered and in pain. She parked in the garage and took the elevator to the third floor, not realizing that floor was under renovation. When the elevator doors slid open, she was startled to find herself facing a brick wall—the doorway had been completely bricked up. Shaken, she took the elevator down to the second floor and walked up a flight of stairs to the doctor's office. While there she had her abscess lanced, but she experienced a reaction to the anesthetic, which made her heart race out of control, creating a feeling of panic. By the time she took the elevator back to the parking garage and collapsed behind the wheel of her car, she was an emotional wreck.

Finishing her story, she took a sip of coffee, thought a minute, then said, "What you're saying about memories makes sense, because last night it dawned on me that the elevator in my dentist's building wasn't the problem at all. Oh, sure, it was unnerving to have those elevator doors open to a brick wall, but what *really* shook me was everything that happened *before* and *after* my elevator ride. In reality, all the anxiety, pain, disorientation, fear, and panic I felt that day were because of my abscessed tooth and drug reaction. And yet for twenty years, I've associated all those feelings with elevators and parking garages. I think just realizing this is going to make a *big* difference in how I feel the next time I need to step into an elevator."

How cool is *that*? Scott keeps a client, Mom keeps her fabulous hairstyle, *and* you and I get a great story about how memories—and mixed-up ones at that—can keep us in an emotional funk.

I think it's kind of scary that what we *believe* about an experience can impact our emotions far more than the experience itself. But it's also kind of freeing, because it means you and I may have more control over our feelings than we ever imagined.

Whether we're deciding what to believe about something that occurred five minutes or five decades ago, the choices we make can impact our emotions—and our peace, joy, and hope—for years to come.

Here are five ways to change the beliefs we attach to the events in our lives:

1. Don't take it personally

When we feel slighted, offended, or hurt, it's easy to assume the worst. My invitation never arrived for the block party. Sure, I can assume my neighbors hate me, but why jump to a conclusion that will probably leave me feeling rejected or angry? Do the neighbors *really* hate me or was my mail delayed? Did someone write my address down wrong? Did the invitation get dropped in the street when I brought in the mail? Why not just stick to the facts? My invitation never arrived and I have no idea why.

And the truth is, we really *don't* know the motives behind much of what people say or do.

I'll never forget an incident that occurred one Sunday over brunch. Several friends and I were seated in a hotel restaurant waiting for service. And waiting. And waiting. When our waiter finally showed up, he flung menus at us and practically barked the specials of the day. When one woman asked for a clean water glass, he rolled his eyes and left without a word. By now my friends and I were highly offended and complaining vehemently to each other. One woman started looking around for a manager. Someone else suggested simply walking out.

About that time our testy waiter returned. On a whim I turned to him and said, "You seem *very* impatient and annoyed and we were wondering why."

His eyes flew open and something in his face seemed to melt. "I *do*? I had no idea. I'm very sorry. I've got the worst migraine and I've taken everything I can think of and I'm still in so much pain I can't think straight. I'm sure the painkillers will kick in soon. If not, I'll probably head home early. Really, I had no idea. I'm so sorry."

After that, he was gracious and attentive and later, when we asked about his headache, he said it was almost gone.

Look, life is hard enough without always assuming the worst. Whenever possible, assume the best. Out of a dozen possible motives behind any action or comment, try to pick one that will create the memory that will leave you nursing the fewest wounds.

2. Don't generalize, catastrophize, or internalize

A friend of mine came home from a dead-end blind date and said, "See? This *always* happens to me."

Kaitlyn misplaced her calendar and stood up a friend for lunch. She winced and confessed, "I just did the most terrible thing in the world!"

Kacie and I were eating fast food in my car when suddenly she groaned and said, "I'm a horrible person!" I said, "Why is that?" She pointed and said, "I just spilled ranch dressing all down the side of the seat." I handed her a napkin and said, "Hannibal Lecter was horrible. You're just sloppy. Trust me, there's a difference."

The truth matters. And when we don't speak the truth—when we generalize, catastrophize, or internalize—the skewed memories that are created can siphon away our peace, joy, and hope for years to come.

3. Be a spin doctor

Something painful happened. Maybe you lost your waistline or your temper or your bread-and-butter client. You failed someone you loved. A friend said something mean. You picked up an old habit. You picked a fight. You picked door number three when all the really *great* prizes were behind door number one.

Is there anything good you can glean from the experience?

Did you learn something? Grow in some way? Did you handle something in a way you could be proud of later? Did you model something healthy for your kids? When it was all said and done, did you keep your integrity intact? If not, did you handle your mistake by eventually seeking accountability or forgiveness or resolution?

We can remember the mistake or the flop or the wound. Or we can remember the growth that occurred as a result. The first memory hurts. The second one heals. The choice is ours.

4. Keep this, toss that

Okay, so about this relationship of mine that went belly-up.

He was the wrong man at the wrong time, but the heart has a mind of its own, doesn't it? And this guy, well, he did have some nice qualities and loveable quirks. (I can't keep calling him "this guy." I think I'm going to call him Skippy.)

Four months after we ended contact, I was frantically pulling together paperwork for my taxes. (Yes, yes, I know it was October. Can you say "extension"?) In fact it was two in the morning and I had six hours to compile everything before going to the accountant, who assured me he had just enough time to get my taxes filed before my extended deadline came and went.

So there I was in the middle of the night, dog tired, pawing through the cardboard box where, every year, I toss anything that comes across my desk sporting any kind of number. The first thing I pulled out was a receipt from Home Depot. Then a check register. Then a bank statement and another receipt, this one for makeup (could that be considered a capital improvement?). Then a plumbing invoice, insurance premium notification, auto license renewal form, a receipt for books from Borders (research), a receipt for coffee from Borders (more research).

I pulled out another piece of paper, took one look, and burst into tears.

I hadn't seen this for a year, not since *last* October when I was facing the same deadline, foraging for tax documents and feeling frantic and overwhelmed. Skippy had spent the afternoon helping me hunt and sort, and before leaving he'd grabbed a sheet of blank paper and a Sharpie, doodled this note, and taped it to my dining room window for inspiration. There were squirrels and hearts and caricatures of each of us. There were tax tips. Across the top he had penned boldly, "I HAVE FAITH IN YOU." Below, he had scrawled the initials IWALYNMW.

I will always love you no matter what.

The next morning I showed up at my folks' place with my receipts neatly totaled and ready to go. We had time for a cup of coffee before I had to leave for the accountant's office, and somewhere between the Splenda and the creamer, I broke down and told them through tears about the note.

If I thought I was going to hear, "Forget about it," I was wrong.

Dad said, "Someone you loved believed in you. That's a good memory, worth hanging on to. Right now it's hard to fathom, but one day you'll be able to look back and remember the gift without reliving the hurt."

Maybe some memories, the good ones, are like cream. Maybe, in time, it's possible to separate the elements, like skimming the fat from the milk, keeping the sweetest parts and tossing the rest.

Keep the good stuff.

Move past the pain.

I believe it can be done. I'm working on it. You work on it too. And if you figure it out before I do, email me, okay? Sometimes a girl needs all the help she can get.

5. Don't be an elephant

Last year someone I care about sent me an email filled with harsh statements and accusations. She was really stressed at the time, and I was pretty sure she didn't mean everything she'd written, but I still felt mad and hurt and livid and betrayed. And did I mention mad?

I composed a fiery response, and toward the end of my message, I actually wrote these words: "I could delete your email, but I'm not going to. I'm going to keep it so that if reconciliation ever becomes a possibility, I can reread your words, rekindle everything I'm feeling right now, and remind myself to say, 'No thanks, I'll pass.'"

Ooops. So much for the verse in Corinthians that says real love doesn't keep a record of wrongs (1 Cor. 13:5).

I realize sometimes there's stuff we need to remember so we can set healthier boundaries or keep from making the same mistake twice. But can't we learn from our mistakes without taking the memories that provoke us to pain or anger and nursing them forever at our breast?

Thank God I never emailed my response to my friend. And it's a good thing. We're friends again and working through the stuff in her life and mine that prompted her to write the things she did.

If elephants have perfect memories, I'm guessing they don't have a lot of friends and they probably don't sleep well at night either. If we're not careful, a "perfect" memory can keep us from getting over a snag in a normally healthy relationship, and it can also rob us of our own happiness, hope, and peace.

When it comes to managing our memories, the stuff we store really *can* determine how we feel. So don't take things too personally. Don't generalize, catastrophize, or internalize. Put a positive spin on things whenever you can. Keep the sweet stuff; toss the pain. And remember to forget a few things now and then.

And if the stuff you forget happens to include the names of your kids and relatives, don't despair. I hear one of the stores in town is running a sale on nametags. . . . If I could only remember which store.

Turn on a Light

- What do you think about the idea that our memories are subjective? Could it be true? Can you think of any examples of this in your life?

- Out of all the "don'ts" discussed in this chapter —don't take things personally; don't general- ize, catastrophize, or internalize; and don't be an elephant—is there one in particular you struggle with?

- Are you being an elephant about something? If you could forget about this thing, would anything in your life or relationships improve?

- What kind of precautions are you willing to take to protect yourself from being influenced or hurt by distorted thoughts, memories, or conclusions?

3

I Went Jogging Once but My Thighs Rubbed So Much My Pantyhose Caught on Fire

A friend of mine—I'll call her Amber—is going through a really tough time. In fact last month she suffered the third in a rapid succession of unrelated emotional blows.

A couple days ago I was with her when she covered her face with her hands and whispered lifelessly through her fingers, "When do I explode?"

I said, "Explode?"

"Explode. From all the pain. When do I just explode?"

Amber wasn't talking about releasing pent-up anger. She was talking about the ultimate broken heart, the final rupture of a heart stretched to the bursting point with hurt.

I thought about her words that night and the next day as I went through the paces of my morning routine, exercising, showering, dressing for the day, packing up my laptop, getting in my car, and heading for one of three local coffee shops where, for the price of a café mocha, I can spend the entire day hanging around and writing without getting escorted off the premises for loitering.

As my car idled at an intersection several blocks from my house, I stopped thinking about my friend for a moment so I could decide which way to turn. By turning right I'd end up in the vicinity of Barnes and Noble and The Place. Turn left and I'd end up at It's a Grind. I turned toward The Place. A moment later, on a whim, I made a U-turn and headed for It's a Grind.

If only hurting hearts could turn on a dime as easily.

I know what my friend is experiencing. She's feeling numb and powerless. Like a surfer who finds herself thrust violently below the surface of the water by one too many crashing waves, my friend is spinning, disoriented, in a world of hurt.

As I drove, I tapped my fingers on the steering wheel. *What to do . . . what to do . . . what to do . . .*

Right now, there's little anyone can do about Amber's circumstances. But her emotions are a different story. *Think . . . think . . . numb and powerless. What's a good elixir for numb and powerless?*

I smacked palm to forehead. Of course!

I knew *exactly* how to help Amber begin to experience a measure of hope and power over her life. The first thing I had to do was get her to agree to dedicate two hours a week for the next couple months. The second thing I needed to do was find a good karate instructor, one who would let her punch stuff.

These boots are made for walkin'

I believe with all my heart that one of the things Amber needs right now is a generous dose of endorphins, adrenaline, and attitude, which is exactly what I needed last year when things went bust with Skippy. I remember that, the day after things ended, I looked at my face in the mirror, looked at my heart on the floor, and strapped on my hiking boots and iPod.

I passed Kaitlyn on my way out the front door. She said, "Where are you going?"

My exact answer was, "I need endorphins, adrenaline, and attitude."

I took to the tree-lined roads around my house, sometimes walking five to seven miles a day, pounding the pavement to the most butt-kicking, attitude-embossed beats and vocals I could find.

Our bodies produce endorphins as a natural painkiller and also to generate a general sense of well-being, even happiness. And sure enough, the endorphins I generated with all that exercise gave me some temporary relief from my pain.

Adrenaline is the hormone our bodies produce that gets us ready to fight or flee danger. And, indeed, the adrenaline coursing through my body convinced me that, one way or another, I would survive.

As for the rock and roll, it pumped my will to live to a new level. I would not merely find a way to survive. I was going to survive *with style*.

When circumstances go awry, our lives can feel out of control and unpredictable. But one thing that doesn't change too much is the way our bodies are wired. I'm not saying stress doesn't take a toll, but for the most part, our bodies work the same the day *after* our heart cracked as the day before. Did you get bad news at work? Are you behind on your mortgage? Did you find the thirty pounds your best friend just lost, leaving you not only jealous but chubbier to boot? None of that changes the fact that if you do certain things, like take a long walk or spend an hour kickboxing, your body *will* reward you with a burst of endorphins and/or adrenaline.

When circumstances reel out of our control, we have a choice. Sure, we can continue feeling like yesterday's dirty laundry stuck in an eternal spin cycle, or we can begin reclaiming control in our life, starting with our very own body.

Fancy meeting you here!

Driving the rest of the way to the coffee shop, I pondered how to find the right martial arts instructor for Amber. Internet? Yellow pages? Word of mouth? And there are so many styles of martial arts. Which one would be the best for her?

Walking into It's a Grind, I ordered coffee, found a corner table, and turned on my laptop. Before long my fingers were flying as I became immersed in completing the chapter you just finished reading on memories. I was so immersed, in fact, that I didn't hear the comment of the man at the table next to me the first time he spoke.

He repeated his question. "Excuse me, is your wireless Internet working?"

I checked. "Nope."

"Thanks. I wondered if something was wrong with my computer. I guess I'll just be patient. I'm sure they'll have it back up and running in a few minutes. I'm Kurt, by the way."

We exchanged introductions and pleasantries. I asked Kurt what he was working on.

"Well, right now I'm updating the class schedule on our website."

"Class schedule?"

"I own a gym here in town. I'm a martial arts instructor."

(Insert dramatic organ chords!)

Kurt and I talked for forty minutes, exchanged cards, and promised to follow up with each other in a few days. That evening, I told Amber everything, about the adrenaline, endorphins, and attitude, about almost heading to a different coffee shop, about the U-turn and Kurt and, most important, that she was going to get to punch stuff, lots of stuff.

She actually smiled. I figured it was a beginning. "Okay," she said. "It's different but, yeah, okay, I'll try it."

Better living through chemistry

I realize this isn't a science class, but grant me a few brief paragraphs to talk about how you can get more mileage out of your body's ability to create mood-altering hormones.

Endorphins, released by our pituitary glands when our bodies are in stress or trauma, block pain and elevate our moods. This is why folks talk about that "runner's high," that wonderful endorphin rush you can experience three-fourths of the way into any long, continuous workout. Running, swimming, cross-country skiing, long-distance rowing, bicycling, aerobics, basketball, and soccer are good examples of endorphin-friendly activities.

But in case—like me—you think exercise is a dirty word, and any time you say it, you have to wash your mouth out with chocolate, you'll be glad to know there are other ways to get your endorphin fix. In fact any time your body is pushed beyond the comfort zone—by physical activity, stress, or even mild pain—endorphins can result. Acupuncture, making love, laughing so hard your sides hurt and you can't catch your breath, even childbirth can all prompt the release of endorphins. Going to a chiropractor or doing yoga or Pilates are also on the list. Even eating chili peppers can release endorphins, which is the premise behind a new product on the market. Sinus Buster is the world's first nasal spray containing hot pepper extract, designed to kick your body into instant endorphin production.

And even though endorphins are short-lived and don't seem to provide a ton of long-term benefits, who cares? Even a temporary burst of endorphins can lessen anxiety and depression, relieve pain, elevate our mood, lower blood pressure, enhance our immune system, *and* remove superoxides, slowing down how fast we age.

Adrenaline, on the other hand, helps our bodies prepare for action in emergency situations, making us stronger and more alert. Danger, noise, excitement, even bright lights, can bring on the adrenaline. So how can you create an adrenaline rush to lift your spirits? Going to a concert, kickboxing, riding a roller coaster, skydiving, wrestling a bear, fencing, or running with the bulls in Pamplona are just a few adrenaline-producing activities you may want to consider.

Or not.

The point is, when you want to feel more alert, energetic, and happy, no matter what your circumstances look like, endorphins and adrenaline are great friends to have on your side.

If you're happy and you know it, nod your head (and if you absolutely have to whine, at least talk fast)

Of course, not *everybody* has as much energy as, say, my friend Kurt. But even couch potatoes can feel better with just a few small body movements. How small?

Think you can manage a nod?

Even small body movements—including smiling and nodding—can influence our mood. People who looked at themselves in a mirror and forced a fake smile reported feeling happier and more hopeful as a result.

And as for the whole nodding thing, people who were asked to read a statement while nodding their heads "yes" scored higher confidence levels in what they were saying than people who were asked to read the exact same statement while shaking their heads "no." In other words, nodding your head up and down while you're talking can boost your own confidence in what you're saying.

One last piece of weird body trivia and then I'll move on, I promise. Here's something else you can do with your body that will make you feel better: talk faster.

This is because talking faster than normal can make you feel happier. (Alvin the Chipmunk should be ecstatic.)

To figure this out, researchers had folks read a series of statements aloud. Sometimes they were asked to read quickly, sometimes slowly. Some of the statements were downers ("I want to go to sleep and never wake up"), while others were inherently exciting ("Wow! I feel great!"). It didn't matter *what* people were being asked to read. Whether the content was depressing or uplifting, just the act of thinking quickly boosted readers' moods, energy, creativity, and confidence. Even thinking sad thoughts at a fast pace made people happier.[2]

My conclusion? The next time you can't untether your emotions from less than pleasant circumstances, try the following.

Repeat the phrase "Iampeacefulhappyandhopeful" ten times as quickly as you can while nodding your head up and down *and* smiling. Yes, yes, I know it's an unusual approach, but what'll it hurt to try? You've got nothing to lose but the blues.

You've lost that lovin' feelin', so maybe it's time to twist and shout

One day I was so sad I could barely stand to be in my own skin. Have you ever felt like that, like even your cells are sad? Normal sadness seems to hover just above your lungs and often feels like something a good heart transplant could cure. But every now and then, I find myself in circumstances that evoke the kind of sadness that even a cardiac surgeon can't address. On those days, I don't need a new heart. I need a whole new body. Forget Dr. House. I need Dr. Frankenstein. And let's hope he's got plenty of spare parts on hand.

Anyway, it was a day just like that, and I was supposed to take my kids to a family cookout at my parents' house, but what I *really* wanted to do was find some far-off destination, hop on a plane, and leave everything behind, including myself. Wouldn't that be great? No heart. No little sad cells. No memories. Nothing.

Airline employee: "Will you be checking any luggage today?"

45

Me: "Nope. I'm not even taking my own body. Although I wouldn't mind a window seat. Are there any available?"

Airline employee: "Security!"

How was I going to get through the day? Ahhh . . . I had an idea. Walking in the front door of my parents' house, the first thing I did was put down the pot of green beans I'd been carrying. The second thing I did was plug in my iPod and docking station and dial up a playlist I'd created for a party my kids gave last fall. The Supremes' "Stop! In the Name of Love," Aretha's "R-e-s-p-e-c-t," and Sister Sledge singing "We Are Family" filled the kitchen.

The next thing I did was dance, and as various family members walked unsuspectingly through the front door, I pulled them into my impromptu kitchen sock hop as well. Russ, Gabriella, Kacie . . .

Now, you have to know something. I did *not* grow up in a dancing family. In fact I wasn't allowed to go to school dances or attend movies either. Or cuss or smoke or chew or drive with boys on the freeway. It was just the way I was raised, and I guess I turned out okay. At least that's what all my therapists tell me.

But now I'm forty-six. So when my folks came into the kitchen and shook their heads in disbelief at all their gyrating offspring, in-laws, and grandkids, well . . . what could they do? Send me to my room?

Actually, they may have shaken their heads in disbelief, but they were smiling at the same time. They had to. It's impossible to hear "Wild Thing" or James Brown's "I Feel Good" without breaking into a grin.

Still, Dad fulfilled his role beautifully as the family patriarch, putting on a scowl and saying, "You kids call that music? That's not music. Glenn Miller. Now *that* was music."

Oh, how I relish what happened next.

Wearing only the faintest of victory smirks, I walked to my iPod and spun a little further into the playlist.

Strains of "Moonlight Serenade" filled the room.

You should have seen his face. When he could raise his jaw enough to speak, he said, "You have *Glenn Miller* on there?"

"I do. Hey, you used to be a dance instructor" (and he did, at Arthur Murray's Dance Studio back in the late forties, making the ban on *my* school dances seem all the more mysterious). "So come on. Give me a dance lesson." And I held my arms wide.

It took a little coaxing, but within minutes, there I was, dancing with my dad to Glenn Miller. My dad is seventy-four now, and I'll bet he hasn't danced in forty years, but his moves were seamless and, with a few tricks of the trade, he made me feel like I almost knew what I was doing too.

But the best part came next.

I turned to my mom and said, "Your turn."

She looked surprised. "Dance? But I don't know how to dance."

"He makes it easy. Go on."

47

My dad took her in his arms. "Moonlight Serenade" drew to a close and the McGuire Sisters started singing "Goodnight Sweetheart." And my parents danced.

I still smile just thinking about it.

Nothing had changed. My circumstances were exactly the same. But at that very moment, my heart didn't hurt. And my cells weren't sad. And, well, life was good.

You and I can't always remove the obstacles in our life or even budge the hungry void left by an unbearable loss, but we *can* tap our toes and flex our muscles and exercise the corners of our mouths. And eventually all that movement creates a stirring in our heart. It can even put a spring in our step.

And on some days, that'll do just fine.

Turn on a Light

- My friend Linda says, "No matter how lethargic I feel, how much I dread it, or how hard I try to procrastinate, the truth is I have *never* finished a walk or a workout with the words, 'Wow, I regret doing this.'" What about you? How do you feel after a walk or workout?

- Get a piece of paper. Write a list of the stuff that's been keeping you from getting your body in motion. Now fold that list into a paper airplane and send it sailing across the room. No, really. Do it. Right now. For real. I'll stop typing until you can get that piece of paper, write your list, make your airplane, and send it sailing.

- Done? Great! See? Even your list of "Reasons I Can't Move" can move. And so can you. Get going. (And if you happen to live in Colorado, you can always get going at Kurt Frankenberg's Freedom School of Martial Arts in Colorado Springs.)

- Why should Alvin and the Chipmunks have all the fun? It's our turn. Repeat the phrase "Iampeacefulhappyandhopeful" aloud ten times as quickly as you can while nodding your head up and down *and* smiling. There. Feel any better?

4

Don't Blame Me—the Voices in My Head Made Me Do It

Midmorning one Saturday, I picked up the phone and called my sister Renee. I was still in my pj's, thinking about looking into the possibility of considering the option of getting out of bed. As soon as she answered, I could tell by her voice that she was about as ready for the day as I was. Sure enough, she admitted, "I haven't even gotten up yet."

"Me neither. But I'm lying here thinking of reasons to get out of bed, and the words that keep coming to mind are 'coffee' and 'leopard-print mini lamp shades.'"

"Leopard is *always* worth getting up for. And what are you planning to do with these leopard-print shades?"

"Put them on the wall chandelier above the fireplace. Which is why we both need to get out of bed, throw on some clothes, and meet at Hobby Lobby in forty-five minutes."

"I can't get there that soon. How about two hours?"

"One hour and that's my final offer."

"Okay. Sure. I'll see you there." She yawned.

"You have no intention of getting up, do you?"

"Actually, no."

"Okay, on the count of three, sit up and put both feet on the floor. One, two, three." I waited. I didn't hear any movement on the other end of the line. "You're not sitting up, are you?"

"Not really."

It was my turn to sigh. "Back when I used to be on the S.W.A.T. team, they gave us training for these kinds of situations. Like for when we had to negotiate with terrorists and disarm suicidal people. So here goes. All right, Renee, I want you to stick one leg out from the covers. Just one. Don't worry about the other leg. We're taking baby steps here. One leg. In fact let's start with just a foot. I know you can do it. One foot. Give it a wiggle, then begin inching it toward the edge of the mattress. . . . You're doin' great . . . don't stop . . . just a few more inches."

"Okay, fine. I'm sitting up."

She sounded so grumpy I knew she was telling the truth.

"Great!" I hopped out of bed.

"I noticed you haven't mentioned coffee," she said accusingly. "You're not nearly as concerned about the coffee as I am, are you?"

"Actually, no. Ever since I've been whitening my teeth, I've cut back."

"That's not a good excuse. I can't hang out with any-one who's not as addicted to coffee as I am. I've had otherwise perfect friendships grind to a complete halt over this very issue."

I shrugged. "Okay, fine. So I buy a few extra tubes of whitening gel. Meet me at Starbucks and then we'll shop for lamp shades. You still need an hour to get ready?"

In the background I heard a car engine start.

"An hour? Are you *nuts*? I can smell that coffee brew-ing already. Get a move on, girl. I'll be there in ten minutes."

Under the influence

What are the things that make us do the things we do?

Sure, coffee and shopping are fun motivators. On more meaningful levels, we're influenced by the people in our lives—husbands, kids, friends, colleagues, and others. Jobs and financial obligations impact our actions, as do past experiences and future goals. And what woman hasn't been driving innocently down the street and found herself lured six blocks out of her way by a garage sale sign promising treasure *and* killer deals to boot?

God can direct our paths too. Remember my un-planned U-turn so I could go to a *different* coffee shop where the man drinking coffee at the next table turned out to be the martial arts instructor I had, just that morning, determined I needed to find? Coincidence? Hardly. God-incident? You bet.

You and I can even be influenced by *that* time of the month, although we'll never *ever* admit it to the men in our lives. After all, if we admitted it, we couldn't hold it against them the next time they do that infuriating thing where they try to win an argument by getting that "I just had an epiphany!" look on their faces, slapping palms to foreheads and saying knowingly, "Hold on a minute. Are you on your *period*?" And the worst part about that very sexist, patronizing inquiry is that, almost every time a man has asked me that question, the answer is yes. What kind of weird coincidence is *that*? But— off the record—apparently you and I *can* be influenced by our cycles. This is why they make T-shirts with the slogan, "They call it PMS because Mad Cow Disease was already taken."

There's something else that has a profound influence on our actions, choices, and even our attitudes. I'm talking, of course, about the voices in our heads.

I'm not schizophrenic and neither am I

No, not those kinds of voices. I'm referring to the running dialogue we have with ourselves. More specifically, the other voice in the conversations we always seem to be having with ourselves—the stuff we tell ourselves when no one else is listening. And don't try to convince me that I'm the only woman who has these kinds of ongoing conversations in her head.

Several weeks ago I went to Home Depot and purchased twenty boxes of Pergo laminate. Wheeling the stack of boxes on a flatbed cart all the way to my car, it dawned on me I was never going to get all this stuff in my 4Runner, which was at that very moment brimming with school backpacks, props for last year's Christmas drama, an industrial-sized can of green beans, two doggie beds, three windshield snow scrapers, several jumper cables, six winter coats, a mesh bag filled with swimsuits and towels, two cases of bottled water, and the cable modem I was supposed to return to the cable company last spring.

After squeezing a mere four boxes of laminate into my truck, I ran out of room, so I wheeled the rest back into the store, went to the customer service desk, and explained my dilemma. The clerk agreed to hang on to the laminate until I could return for it, gave me a claim receipt, and sent me on my way.

The next day I went back and presented my claim receipt to a different clerk. A moment later, a man in an orange apron was wheeling a cartload of twenty boxes of laminate toward the store exit.

Twenty boxes.

They were mistakenly giving me my full purchase, even though I'd already taken four of the boxes home with me.

I did the math. At twenty-four dollars a box, that was nearly a hundred dollars of laminate. Okay, *fine*. Stolen laminate. Nevertheless, unbidden thoughts flew through my head. Did I need extra laminate? If not, what would happen if I tried to exchange them later for something I could use? Or bring them back for a cash refund?

As I was recognizing the presence of these embarrassing-to-admit questions, my conscience spoke up. It said, *Have you lost your ever-lovin' mind? You don't want four extra boxes of laminate. And you don't want the hundred bucks you could get by returning them to the store. What you want is a clear conscience. You want to be a person of integrity. You want God's blessing on your life. And you're not going to give all that up by walking out the door with something that doesn't belong to you.*

I said to the man in the orange apron, "There are twenty boxes on that cart. There should be only sixteen."

As he unloaded the four extra boxes, the man was all smiles. And he couldn't stop complimenting me. "Thank you for being so honest! Most people wouldn't have said a word. Thank you. Thanks for saying something. An honest person. Wow! I'm impressed."

"Well," I winced, "I did *think* about it . . . for a split second. But then I told myself, *Hey, that's not who you are, and it's definitely not who you wanna be.* Which is why I spoke up, but it actually crossed my mind. Yeah, I know. Surprised me too. Crazy, the stuff that'll go through your head. Isn't it crazy?"

The man never answered. In fact he'd stopped speaking to me altogether, and he wasn't smiling anymore. Apparently his appreciation for honesty went only so far. Our conversation was over.

But that's okay. I figured the conversation that *really* mattered was the one that had gone on between me and, well, me!

Speak up!

What we tell ourselves *does* matter. When we're faced with moral dilemmas or temptations, what we say to ourselves can make the difference between living small or walking tall.

What we tell ourselves when we're discouraged is just as critical. When the light at the end of the tunnel is faint (or even gone!) and our circumstances seem tough or sad or hopeless, what we say to ourselves *really* matters, because while temptation can be fleeting, sometimes discouraging circumstances can go on for days or months or even years. Do the voices in our head inspire us toward hope and happiness and contentment and life? Or do they leave us feeling even worse than before they piped up?

I wish I knew about this stuff only from reading books. Unfortunately, this is where I live. All the stuff I'm writing about in this chapter—and the chapters before this one and the chapters yet to come—is what I do to encourage myself when I get discouraged, which happens a lot. Meaning I get plenty of practice.

And what I've noticed in my life is this: when I get discouraged, there are several different ways I can "talk" to myself, some of which make me feel better and some of which make me feel worse. I'm going to tell you what all of those voices sound like in just a minute. But first, here's something else I've noticed: most of the time, I can choose pretty much the "voice" I want to use.

And that means you get to choose too.

We're not wired differently, you and I. We might wear different shades of lipstick or listen to different styles of music on our iPods, but the same resources that work for me will work for you as well. You and I *can* have happy, fabulous lives even when our circumstances look dim. And one of the ways we can start *today* to make that happen is by being intentional about whom we hang out with in our own head!

Here are some of the voices on my own personal roster, and I'll bet you've got the same ones at your disposal as well:

Our inner Eeyore

Eeyore, the old grey Donkey, stood by the side of the stream, and looked at himself in the water.

"Pathetic," he said. "That's what it is. Pathetic."

He turned and walked slowly down the stream for twenty yards, splashed across it, and walked slowly back on the other side. Then he looked at himself in the water again.

"As I thought," he said. "No better from this side. But nobody minds. Nobody cares. Pathetic, that's what it is."[3]

Sometimes I wonder if Eeyore was miscast as a donkey when he should have been a night owl. I say this because, more often than not, my inner Eeyore pipes up in the middle of the night when we both should be sleeping. He's yammering, and I'm tossing and turning.

This happened just last night.

Day before yesterday I went to the dentist. It was on a Friday afternoon, and by evening most of the dental block had worn off. But sometime Saturday it dawned on me that there was a lingering numbness on one side of my chin. It didn't worry me too much until late last night, when worrisome thoughts eventually morphed into a mild panic. Now, *rational* thoughts might have gone something like this: *First thing Monday morning, call the doctor. In the meantime, just relax. Maybe there's temporary nerve trauma that will eventually heal. Worse case scenario, I guess you'll never be able to use the right corner of your chin to read anything written in Braille.*

But Eeyore isn't into reason. Eeyore is into pity parties, fatalistic thinking, and hysteria. So by 3:00 a.m. not only was I feeling sorry for myself, I was feeling victimized and helpless *and* envisioning myself learning to cope with total facial paralysis.

What might *your* inner Eeyore sound like?

"You can't do it, so why even try?"

"You're unlovable."

"Something bad is going to happen. I just know it!"

"This is as good as it's ever going to get."

"You don't deserve better than this."

"You can't fix your marriage, so why even try?"

"You're always going to be fat!"

"Everyone else but you has their life together."

"You're never going to feel better."

Our inner Eeyores don't need any prompting. They usually show up on their own, and they're often the first guys on the scene.

But we don't *have* to listen to them. We *do* have other options.

Our inner Grandma

Last night, shortly after hitting the mild panic zone, I decided to make a conscious effort to gag Eeyore and adopt a new persona for my inner voice. I chose Grandma.

You know the voice. "There, there. Everything's going to be all right. It's late. You're exhausted. Everything's going to look much brighter in the morning. You're going to be okay. It's all fine. Take a deep breath. That's it. Good girl. Again, deep breath. All right, now wipe those tears and let's have some homemade chicken soup, shall we?"

Grandma is soothing. She doesn't always offer a ton of solutions, but she does pat your hand a lot and give you cookies.

And sometimes that's exactly what a girl needs.

Our inner Coach

When we need comfort, we go to Grandma's house. But when we need strategy, it's time to turn to our inner Coach. Giving ourselves an energizing pep talk takes more energy than giving ourselves, say, a plate of warm cookies, but it's worth it!

A few months ago I got an email from a reader named Pam. She wrote: "Last year we were in a real financial bind. On second thought, it was more like a vise grip. My husband had just been laid off and I was three months pregnant. For weeks I moped around the house, prophesying doom and gloom. Then one night I looked at my husband and he looked so dejected it felt like my heart snapped in two. I started massaging his shoulders and telling him how smart and talented he was. I told him we'd get through this, and that in the meantime we would cancel cable TV, eat at home, and rent out the spare room for a semester (easily done since we live in a college town). That week I cleaned out the garage and put a bunch of stuff for sale on eBay, eventually bringing in more than a thousand dollars. Two months later he was offered a position with a former competitor. He makes exactly what he made before, but he likes his boss better and he commutes half as far. Best yet, the whole thing taught me how to be an encourager, something I'd always admired in other people but had a hard time nurturing in myself."

What a great transition from Eeyore to Coach! Pam made the shift for her husband, but my guess is that now she's also more aware how to make that shift for herself.

What about you? My guess is that you can get pretty passionate when it comes to encouraging and motivating people you love, whether it's your best friend who is upset because she can't lose fifty pounds or your daughter who is having a hard time finding a summer job. Can you get just as passionate when it comes to encouraging and motivating yourself?

Our inner Grateful Chick

Sometimes I'll be puttering along, half-engaged in a conversation with my inner Eeyore. Sometimes I won't even realize that he's puttering along next to me. I'll just be vaguely preoccupied with mulling over all the nagging negative details of my life. *Sheesh. Tax time again. Great! You'd better look for that extension form earlier this year instead of on April 14 like you usually do. Which reminds me, did you ever call the dermatologist about that dry, flaky patch on your nose? Of course not. What are you waiting for? An act of Congress? Pick up the phone tomorrow, will you puhleese? And your renters move out in two months. Don't forget. You'll have some bills then, baby, yes you will. What if the carpet needs replacing? That could be a couple grand right there. Where's that money going to come from? It's not like you haven't had time to save. You could have planned ahead, you know. Other people plan ahead. Other people even have savings accounts. Oh, yes, they do. You're the only one who doesn't.* (Sigh.) *Ohmigosh, did you just catch a glimpse of yourself in that mirror? Packing on a few pounds around the middle, aren't you? And you've even been exercising regularly. Must be the age thing. I read an article about that, you know. The older you get, the less your body responds to exercise and diet. You can't do the same things you did last year and expect the same results. You're going to have to sweat more and eat less than ever before just to slow the ballooning process. But look, at least your lips aren't fat. They're thinner than ever. That top one has practically disappeared altogether. Wonder where it went? Maybe the same place your breasts go when you lie on your back. I mean, what's that all about? The minute you get horizontal, poof, they're gone. Next time you lie down, maybe you should see if you can find them. You've never checked your armpits, have you? Try your armpits. I'll bet you anything you'll find 'em there.*

I mean, these aren't always conscious thoughts. Just this distracted running monologue. (*Please* tell me you do the same thing. I'm spilling my guts assuming other people do this too, but as you hold this book in your hands, there are probably fourteen thousand other readers and several dozen psychologists reading that last paragraph and saying to themselves, *I used to be able to relate to her, but not anymore. She's not right. The girl's just not right in the head.*)

My point is the whole Eeyore thing gets to be a habit. Not a choice, just a habit. And whenever Eeyore is on auto-mutter like this, I'm not necessarily feeling upset, so it might not dawn on me to turn to Grandma. I may not be seeking strategies, so I don't think about bringing in the Coach. I'm just absentmindedly going through my day, answering email, making dinner, taking my kids to the bookstore, tossing a load of laundry in the machine, driving to the post office. And Eeyore's auto-mutter becomes my background noise, my soundtrack. No wonder at day's end I'm weary of soul as well as limb.

But . . . knowing all this, I'm getting better and better at catching myself. And as soon as I realize what's going on, I'm quick to pull up hard on the reins, bringing Eeyore to a screeching halt and replacing him with . . . drum roll please . . . Grateful Chick.

When I decide to speak to myself in *this* mode, I always begin by talking about the day and the clouds and the mountains. Don't ask me why, I just do. And at the beginning, it feels like I'm faking it. But I keep talking anyway and before long I find myself passionate about every word.

Here's what Grateful Chick sounds like: *It's a beautiful day.* (Sigh.) *The clouds are fluffy, the sun is shining* (yawn), *and I'm surrounded by gorgeous mountains. Look at those mountains. Honestly, I live in the most beautiful spot in the world. And my kids are happy and healthy. And I've got really amazing friends, every one of them. And a roof over my head. I've even got work to do. Fun work. So many people I know are between jobs right now, but I've got work. And, really, now that I think about it, I'm incredibly blessed. I realize that, Lord. I'm blessed. I have a relationship with you. And I have a great life. I really do. And, sure, sometimes I get down about stuff, but the bottom line is that everything is okay. And I'm grateful, truly grateful. You've given me so much. I don't want to lose sight of that. I really don't. Sure, there have been heartaches and disappointments along the way, and sometimes things don't turn out at all the way I plan. But you keep me in the palm of your hand even then, don't you? And somehow we get through it together. Have I said lately how much I ap-*

preciate you? Because I do, very much. And I'm grateful for life—my life. I've got a roof over my head and work to do and people to love who love me back and you in my heart. It doesn't get better than this. Thank you. I mean it. Thank you.

Try it. If it doesn't change the way you feel about your life, email me and I'll send you a gift card for a cup of coffee at Starbucks. Because listening to your inner Grateful Chick will make a difference. It really will.

Our inner Intercessor

Every now and then I get so frustrated with my circumstances that I can't seem to pull out of a blue funk no matter what I do. I don't want warm cookies or pep talks. I don't want to thank God for my life because I don't even want to *think* about my life. I'm just frustrated and grumpy and I have every intention of staying that way, thankyouverymuch.

Does this ever happen to you? If not, do me a favor, okay? *You* write a book on this subject, and I'll be first in line to buy a copy. I promise.

But in the meantime, I'll tell you what I do when I feel this way. I start thanking God for stuff going on in the lives of people I love. And I ask him to bless these folks too. I talk to him about needs in their lives and I thank him for meeting those needs. Because even when I'm too grumpy to believe God can do something cool in my life, I'm never too grumpy to believe God can do something cool in the lives of, for example, my kids.

I had this kind of prayer for Kaitlyn the other day. I was driving in my car and I asked God to bless her with a really wonderful husband and marriage. And then I spent a long time praying for each of my kids, Kaitlyn and Kacie, asking God to intervene in this little thing or that one, thanking him for both of these really amazing girls. I thanked him for Gabriella, Isaac, Hunter, and Connor. And for my friend Linda as she's writing a truly evocative book about what can happen in our lives when we dwell on the healing images crafted so beautifully for us in the Bible.

And by the time I pulled into my driveway, guess what? My grumpies were gone. Vanished. Disappeared. I didn't know where they'd gone and, to be honest, it didn't matter. They could have gone to my armpits to spend a little time with my breasts for all I cared. The important thing was that, by changing the tone and content of my inner dialogue, I had given myself a new lease on life.

Kind of like leopard-print lamp shades. Only cheaper.

Turn on a Light

- Think about the inner voice you hear most of the time. What does she sound like?

- Have you noticed that some people are more negative, belittling, or judgmental about themselves than others? What factors influence the thoughts we choose or the way we tend to speak to ourselves? What factors, events, or people have influenced the inner voice you use most often?

- If you were having a really bad day, how might you go about finding something positive to think about, or something to be grateful for?

- Philippians 4:8 says, "Finally, brothers, whatever is true, whatever is noble, whatever is right, whatever is pure, whatever is lovely, whatever is admirable— if anything is excellent or praiseworthy—think about such things." Does this verse give you any new thoughts or insights?

5

Peace, Joy, Hope:
Now Playing at a Theater Near You

There's something about a good scary movie. Remember the horror movie hostess, Elvira? Actress Cassandra Peterson created the character back in 1981 for the show *Elvira, Mistress of the Dark*, and even today her portrayal of the Gothed-out bombshell remains her most requested role.

I loved the show. Elvira was vampy and campy, and the B-movies she introduced each week were the kind of scary movies that could give you thrills and chills without leaving you emotionally maimed for life.

Unlike some *other* movies I know of.

The first time I saw previews for *The Descent*, I leaned over to my friend Linda and said emphatically, "Okay, *there's* a movie I'll never see. Just the previews are enough to send me into therapy."

I've already confessed that my memory is so bad I can't recall the names of my children, so it shouldn't come as any surprise that two weeks later, when my friend Russ suggested we see *The Descent*, I shrugged and said, "Sure."

At the end, when the credits were rolling, I turned to Russ to say something and couldn't. My jaw was so fatigued from two hours of clenching that it refused to budge. There were also bloody fingernail moons in both of my palms and I felt like throwing up. Other than that, it was an enjoyable afternoon.

Getting ready for bed that night, I looked out my window into the forest around my house and felt my hair stand on end. In the movie, seven adventurous women had trekked through woods *exactly* like mine before descending into the cavernous bowels of an uncharted cave for a weekend of spelunking with the girls. (Trust me, they should have gone to the mall.) I won't tell you how many lived to tell the story. I won't even tell you what happened while they were down there (can you say "bloodbath"?).

What I *will* tell you, however, is that after watching that movie, it was impossible to look into the woods around my house without seeing the luminous darting shapes of the carnivorous critters these women eventually encountered. It was difficult getting a lot of the movie's images out of my head.

That night I slept with all the lights on.

And music playing.

I did the same thing the next night.

And the next.

On the fourth night, I decided I could handle sleeping in a dark room again. I fell asleep with only minimal trauma. A few hours later, I got my usual 3:00 a.m. bladder call and made it safely and sanely across my darkened room to the bathroom. Returning to bed, however, was an entirely different story.

I turned off the bathroom light, took three steps toward my bed, and stopped. I could see right away this wasn't going to work at all. There was a problem, a big problem.

I studied the situation. There had to be *something* I could do that would get me safely where I needed to be.

In the end, I had to leave the bathroom light on, run to my bed, turn on the lamp next to my bed, run back to the bathroom, turn off the bathroom light, walk to within three feet of my bed, *leap* onto my bed to stay beyond the grasp of anything reaching for me from beneath the bed skirt, and then turn off my nightstand lamp.

Don't laugh. *Anything* could have been under that bed.

There's no question about it. Images are powerful things.

Picture this

Years ago, while going through a very difficult time in my life, I couldn't seem to shake the image of myself as broken. Several times a day my words to myself were, *I'm broken and I'll never be whole again.*

One day my mom said hesitantly, "I had a dream about you last night."

I perked up. "Really?" My mom is very intuitive. A dream? I was very interested in what she had to say.

She nodded. "But I wasn't going to tell you . . . I didn't want it to discourage you."

I prodded, and here is the image that she shared with me: "In my dream there were cracks all over your face. Not *bleeding* cracks but cracks, like a vase that has been dropped and glued back together. But you weren't sad . . . you were laughing. Just like you used to. And then I heard a voice, and it said, 'This is as good as it gets.' So that was it, but I didn't want to tell you, because I didn't want it to discourage you . . ."

"But I was laughing, right?" I was so excited that I interrupted her. "In the dream you said I was laughing?"

"Yes."

"And I wasn't sad anymore."

"No, you weren't sad."

I started to smile. "Mom, that dream doesn't discourage me. It *encourages* me!"

And indeed it did.

I wasn't afraid of scars. What I couldn't take any more was the pain and sadness. But if she had seen me *laughing* . . .

After that I stopped picturing myself as broken and replaced the image in my mind with the one my mother had painted for me. For me, that new picture represented future healing and happiness. It gave me hope.

It would be many months, a few years even, before my mom's dream came completely true, but it did come true. And I have no doubt that the beautiful image she gave me that day was a powerful factor in bringing about the healing that I eventually embraced.

Seeing is believing

Pretty much everybody seems to agree that the images we hold in our mind really do influence not only how we feel but also what happens next in our real world. Most pastors, psychologists, researchers, motivational speakers, and even oncologists agree. The movies we play in the theater of our mind can change our emotions, our choices, our relationships, our future, and our health. I guess what people don't always agree on is why.

Some New Agers claim that our mental images command "the universe" to send us whatever we're imagining. Other folks say it's as simple as the fact that what we imagine tells our brains and bodies what to do. For instance, whether you *try* to trip as you walk across a stage on your way to give a speech—or whether you're so afraid of tripping that you can't stop picturing yourself stumbling over your own feet on your way to the microphone—you've just increased your chances of goin' down.

And when it comes to our emotions? If we entertain sad, hopeless images, we tend to feel sad and hopeless. If we entertain images of peace and hope, we feel peace and hope.

71

Even Peter Pan knew that sometimes to get to where you wanna be, not even pixie dust is enough. To *really* get moving, you've got to throw in some happy thoughts as well.

I'm a boat, a very big boat

I spoke with a woman last week who feels very powerless at the moment. Becky's marriage is in crisis and her husband told her two weeks ago he may file for divorce. At the same time her closest friend was diagnosed with ovarian cancer.

Becky said, "I feel like a rowboat drifting in the middle of the ocean, except my oars are gone and I'm completely at the mercy of the waves and currents around me. Honestly, I don't know if I'll ever be okay again."

How do we keep circumstances—particularly the ones out of our control—from blowing us one way and then the other on the sea of life?

Here's what I think. I think that if we *picture* ourselves as aimless, oarless rowboats at the mercy of every wave and current that comes our way, that's pretty much how it's going to turn out.

This book is about finding some inner core of calm, joy, and hope that stays fairly consistent no matter what's happening around us. And one of the ways I'm convinced you and I can find what we're seeking is by making sure the images we hold in our head are images of health, happiness, and hope rather than powerlessness, rejection, or despair.

72

What if, instead of imagining herself as a powerless craft at the mercy of the elements, Becky tweaked the picture a little? What if she began thinking of herself as an aircraft carrier, powered by nuclear-fueled engines and nineteen-ton propellers? Sure, the waves and weather around her will impact her journey, making it at any given time interesting or frightening or beautiful, but she's not powerless. No matter what happens, she's going to be okay, because her course isn't determined by what's happening on the outside, but by what she's got on the *inside*.

Just when you thought it was safe to go back into the water . . .

During the same painful season in my life that I mentioned earlier, I sought professional help from a wonderful counselor. A former pastor, this wise man counseled with sound psychological advice, biblical principles, and prayer. John really helped me make sense of my life during a confusing, crazy time.

One day as he was praying for me, an image came into his mind. He described to me what he was seeing: "There's someone floating under the water. She's wearing a helmet and jumpsuit, like she's been skydiving and crashed into the ocean by mistake. I can't see her face, but she's lifeless. She's not dead but stunned, as from a great shock, perhaps from her fall from the sky. She's injured too . . . there was a shark, and she was attacked when she fell from where she belonged . . . and now she's missing a leg. But she's not dead, just in shock . . ."

As he spoke, I began to cry. I had never jumped out of an airplane or been undersea in my life, but the emotions his vision evoked were dead on. For many years, I'd *felt* stunned and bleeding, immersed in a hostile environment where I didn't belong and certainly wasn't equipped to survive.

As he continued praying, the image he was watching began to change. He said, "Now I see the same person. She's swimming. She's not wearing skydiving gear anymore but a wet suit and oxygen tank, and she's got a prosthetic leg. She's swimming happily, exploring the ocean floor. She's adapted to this environment, and she's going to be all right."

I groaned. As far as I was concerned, this wasn't great news. What I *wanted* to hear was that Navy Seals arrived posthaste, rescuing this poor woman from the briny sea and returning her to the sky where she belonged. I hated that she was still immersed in circumstances she didn't choose. Her environment hadn't changed at all. What was up with *that*?

Still . . . somehow, she had adapted. She was equipped. She was surviving, yes, but more than that, she was exploring. She was happy. She was going to be all right.

As I continued striving for health and healing, I tucked this image into my growing repertoire of new-and-improved images to hang on to.

I'll be the first to admit that sometimes you and I feel broken or powerless or stunned and displaced. And when we do, we can let the way we feel dictate the way we view ourselves. *Or* we find a new image to hang on to.

Cracked and scarred . . . but laughing.

Tossed by stormy seas . . . but still navigating with inner strength and power.

Immersed in circumstances we didn't choose . . . but equipped, adapting, and thriving.

When it comes to the images we entertain in our mind, there's something to be said for the old adage we've all heard a million times: sometimes what we see really *is* what we get.

Turn on a Light

- If you could describe a picture that represents who you are and how your life feels currently, what would that picture look like?

- Describe an image that makes you feel peaceful. How about happy? How about hopeful?

- Why do these images evoke these feelings in you?

6

Some Days It's Not Worth Chewing through the Restraints

Some days you can't win for losing.

Not long ago I had to catch an afternoon flight for an overnight business trip. Deciding to leave my car in a commuter parking lot near my house, I drove there, locked my car, and lugged my overnight bag onto a shuttle headed for the airport.

As the van pulled out of the parking lot, I glanced out the window and spotted a sign saying, "Cars Left Longer Than 24 Hours Will Be Towed."

I tapped the driver on the shoulder. "What's up with that? I thought I could park here overnight. Does that sign mean twenty-four hours from *now* or twenty-four hours as in *the end of today*?"

He merely shrugged.

I picked up my cell phone, called my sister Michelle, and said, "Help!"

After hearing about my dilemma, Michelle assured me that, sometime before midnight, she would snag my spare car key off the kitchen hook and retrieve my car.

I don't know why these things happen to me. Well, maybe I do. I don't always plan ahead. For instance, I knew an airport shuttle came by this particular location but hadn't phoned ahead to ask about any restrictions. I guess flying by the seat of your pants doesn't necessarily get you to the airport drama-free.

Recently, though, I had done *something* timely I could be proud of. Just that morning I'd been at the Department of Motor Vehicles renewing the registration on Kaitlyn's car and, lo and behold, I'd gone ahead and renewed mine at the same time, even though it wasn't due for several months. This was amazing, because, for the first time in my life, I wasn't renewing my car registration six months late with a ticket in my hand.

Sitting in the shuttle, speeding down Interstate 25 toward the airport, I tried to hang on to the glow of that small success instead of thinking about my miscalculation at the shuttle lot.

The rest of my trip went without incident, and when I was deposited back at the parking lot the following afternoon, Michelle met me there to drive me home.

"Thanks for picking me up . . . and for getting my car last night. You really helped me out of a bind," I said as

I settled into the passenger seat of her car and clicked on my seat belt.

Michelle raised one eyebrow and grinned.

I groaned. "What? What happened? Something happened, didn't it?"

She started to laugh. Apparently what had happened was this: The previous night when Michelle had pulled into the parking lot, it was practically empty except for two cars parked side by side. One was an SUV that, in the fluorescent glow of the streetlight, looked black, not green like mine. The car parked next to it was a police car.

Michelle looked hopefully for another car in the lot that might have been mine before driving slowly toward the two officers circling the dark SUV. Parking her car, she looked closer and sighed. The SUV wasn't black after all. It *was* green.

Still, she assured herself that the officers were probably doing a routine check of local parking lots and that there was nothing about my anonymous 4Runner that had caused them any concern.

She got out of her car.

One of the officers shined a flashlight in her face. "Karen Linamen?" (I figure it's *never* a good sign when they're looking for you by name.)

Introducing herself, Michelle launched into an explanation about the airport shuttle and the surprise twenty-four-hour parking rule. But before she could finish, the officer interrupted her.

"These are stolen plates," he said matter-of-factly. "We've got a tow truck on the way and we're impounding this car."

Michelle blinked. "Stolen plates? What do you mean?"

"They don't match up with what we have on the computer."

"But she renewed them today. Maybe it's not on the computer yet."

He frowned. "Renewed them? Why would she do that? They don't expire for another two months."

"Hard to believe, I'll admit. Even *harder* to believe if you knew her. But wait, I can prove it." Michelle nodded toward my car. "She *never* cleans out her car, so that means the paperwork is probably right here, somewhere on the floor of the car. Can I check?"

A moment later she found the paperwork, tucked between a Styrofoam coffee cup from McDonald's and three ice scrapers.

The officers canceled the tow truck.

Nevertheless, it was a *very* close call.

If at first you don't succeed . . .

Don't you *hate* it when you try to stay on the right side of the law . . . and almost get arrested anyway? What about when you diet for a week . . . and *still* gain three pounds? And what about the day you racked up a hundred dollars in bounced check fees because you forgot to record the check you wrote for the registration fee for that seminar promising to teach you how to get out of debt? Oh, you never did that? I guess that was me.

But something I hate even more is when I do everything I can to stay upbeat and positive and hopeful and happy and confident, and I *still* have a really down day. There's no way around it. Some days—in my ongoing quest to free my emotions from the tyranny of my circumstances—I do all the right things but with none of the right results:

I prune and groom my memories.

I bungee jump (or at least go for an energetic walk about the block) to pump up my endorphins and adrenaline.

I muzzle my inner Eeyore and say encouraging, positive things to myself.

I stop entertaining images of myself as broken or undesirable or overwhelmed, and picture myself as a strong and beautiful woman, loved and embraced by an even stronger and more beautiful God.

. . . and my emotions are *still* in the toilet.

This book is about hanging on to peace, joy, and hope even in the middle of circumstances that are trying, tedious, or tragic. But some days peace, joy, and hope seem to evade us no matter *what* we do.

We *want* to free our emotions from being strapped to our circumstances, but some days it hardly seems worth chewing through the restraints.

What's a girl supposed to do *then*?

Question 1: What do these feelings tell me about my circumstances?

When I have a bad day despite my grandest efforts, I ask myself four questions. The first one is simple: What do these feelings tell me about my circumstances?

It's easy to think, *I'm* feeling *hopeless, so that must mean my circumstances are truly hopeless.* Or *I'm* feeling *sad, so my life must be truly tragic.* Or *I'm* feeling *overwhelmed, so my life must be even more unmanageable than I'd imagined.*

But are feelings and circumstances *really* connected? The truth is most of the time our emotions don't say *anything* about the severity or triviality of our circumstances. Some folks experience hope and triumph during the most tragic times in their lives, while others feel despair over the slightest setback. Our emotions can nose-dive because we didn't get enough sunlight, our blood sugar is askew, or we're functioning on three hours of sleep.

Considering this, is your bad mood *really* the most accurate indicator of the severity of your circumstances?

Question 2: Am I tired or hungry or getting ready to . . . you know?

Have you ever felt lethargic and depressed, and then you eat a long overdue meal and suddenly the world is right again?

Or what about feeling distraught and overwhelmed, getting a good night's sleep, and waking up the next morning calm and confident?

And I won't even *talk* about feeling weepy and annoyed, starting your period, and suddenly feeling like your ol' capable, gracious self again.

Actually, when stuff like this happens, I'm relieved. I realize, *Wow! So my life isn't really falling apart! My circumstances aren't as tragic and hopeless as I thought they were. I should probably cancel that call to Dr. Kevorkian because, as it turns out, all I really needed was a little protein or some shut-eye or to wait a few days until I got my period. How simple was that?*

After four decades of this kind of thing, I'm finally catching on. Now, whenever my circumstances seem overly daunting and my emotions feel out of control, I stop and ask myself if a piece of cheese, a nap, or a little patience will make all the difference in the world. And if the answer is yes, I know exactly what to do with all my scary feelings.

Nothing.

I stop trying to analyze my life, solve the problems of the world, or make any decisions. I don't come to earth-shattering conclusions. I don't try to set anyone straight, confront anything, or attempt to resolve any longstanding disagreements. I chill, eat right, and turn in early. Because sometimes we don't need a psychologist's couch to solve all our wild emotions. Sometimes all we need is a couch.

Question 3: Is there something I need to grieve?

Getting over a broken heart is almost always a two-steps-forward-one-step-back kind of thing. And it was no different for me.

A year ago I floundered in depression as I found myself faced with the impossible task of freeing my wounded heart from a terminally broken relationship. If my circumstances were the *Titanic*, my emotions felt like a battered rowboat on the surface of the water, *chained* to the *Titanic*. Hacksaw in hand and salt in my eyes, could I set myself free before being pulled under for good?

I walked five miles a day. I gave myself pep talks. I reinvented my looks. I even edited his name on my cell phone so that whenever he called (and he called frequently and still does, although only heaven knows why), the words "Big Jerk" would show up on my screen.

Some days all that stuff worked. Other days it didn't.

One day, during a summer thunderstorm, I flung open my bedroom window, sat cross-legged on my bed, and listened to "Refuge" by Vas, one of the most haunting songs I know. With my windows open like that, the stormy weather seemed to transform my room, and I felt immersed in the elements. The air I breathed felt cool and damp, my room smelled like earth and rain, and at times I could barely hear the music over the thunder and the noise of the rain pelting the forest.

I was immersed in thought as well, but to say that I was thinking of the person I'd loved would be an understatement. What I was *really* doing was experiencing the memory of his presence and the reality of his absence with my entire body. At that moment, even my skin felt different.

To an outsider, it might have looked like I was wallowing in sadness. But I knew the truth. In holding my breath and swimming just below the surface of my sorrow, I was searching for a portal, a corridor, just like my window was a corridor to the storm outside. My skin stretched and tingled as if to give way, and I felt a sense of anticipation, as if any moment I might break through to the other side.

Sometimes there is an invisible veil between us and what we long for. That day, in the mist of the steady rain, that veil seemed to take on shape and substance, as if the elements that usually kept it hidden were being washed away. It felt close, both earthy and ethereal. And I couldn't help but feel that, if it could be seen, perhaps it could be penetrated, like a membrane, like a birth. Employing all my senses, I drew as near as I could, then nearer still, yearning to break through to the other side.

I think grieving is a baptism of sorts. Submerged, we swim below the surface of our sorrow, searching for portals, for treasures lost, for the way back home.

Look, I'm all for rising above our circumstances. But sometimes, before we can rise, we need to grieve. Eventually the urge for air and light and life forces us to the surface, and we stay there a little while before diving again. But soon our hours beneath the surface grow shorter and less frequent. Then one day it dawns on us that the blue world of grief has stopped calling our name altogether.

The next time your heart can't seem to rise above your circumstances no matter how hard you try, ask yourself if there's something you need to grieve. Grief is a world all its own, and your time spent there can be painful and precious all at once. At the same time, while pilgrimage is inevitable, residency is ill-advised. So the next time you find yourself swimming below the surface of your sorrow, use your time well. Do what you need to do, but keep reaching for the surface. Air and light and life are waiting for you there.

Question 4: Is it time to stop beating myself up over this?

I imagine we've all gotten phone calls from friends who have just experienced a temporary setback and need a little TLC. And who can blame them? It's easy to feel discouraged when you've been working hard to overhaul a part of your life, and then something happens that makes you feel like you're back where you started.

Usually the comments I hear go something like this:

"I *thought* I was doing better, but I guess I was wrong."

"Oh, great, I'm right back where I started."

"Three weeks of hard work down the drain."

"I feel kinda down today . . . I guess my depression's back."

Last month a friend confessed, "Six months ago I was upset over some really devastating events in my life and started drinking almost every night just to get to sleep. Finally I decided to get a grip on things and hadn't had any alcohol in several months, but last night I was feeling stressed and had a glass of wine. Now I'm starting over from scratch *and* I feel like a big fat failure. Why should I even bother?"

I've experienced clinical depression in the past. On days I feel a little blue—not clinically depressed but just down in the dumps—it's easy to think, *Oh, great, here I go again!*

You know what I want to say to all these people, myself included? Knock it off!

Sometimes it's not about relapse or failure or even starting from scratch. Sometimes it's just a bad day. It happens. (Just ask singer Daniel Powter.) It'll happen again. Don't make it bigger than it is. Forget it and move on.

Setbacks, bad days, and even interludes in the deep end of the sea of grief are going to happen. We can count on them. But we don't need to stay there forever. And we don't have to let such moments today diminish the good stuff we can expect out of life or ourselves tomorrow or the next day or the day after that.

The next time you have a day when you can't seem to get on top of things no matter how hard you try, relax. Don't panic. Take a deep breath. Tomorrow will be a better day.

Turn on a Light

- As a general rule, do you take setbacks in stride or do you tend to panic?

- If one of your friends were mercilessly beating herself up about something or overreacting to a temporary setback, what would you say to encourage her? Can you do the same for yourself?

- What's the best way you can think of to pick yourself up and keep going after a setback?

- Do you do the simple things, like eating regularly and getting enough sleep, that can keep you from feeling down and discouraged when there's no reason to feel that way?

7

Never Take a Laxative and a Sleeping Pill on the Same Night

Life is filled with choices. I made one the other day. Out of about ten thousand books at Barnes and Noble, I picked one off the top shelf. It seemed like a good idea at the time.

I was at the bookstore with a couple of friends. We'd brought our laptops and books and were drinking coffee and working and studying. Pretty mild-mannered stuff, if you ask me. Nothing all that exciting, certainly nothing that would get a person escorted out of a bookstore.

All right, fine. No one *actually* gets kicked out of Barnes and Noble in this story, but I do think the management considered it.

Anyway, Linda, Russ, and I had been working for several hours when Linda got a phone call and stepped outside to talk on her cell. In need of a good stretch, I decided to browse a bit, ending up in the aisle with the books on sexuality and relationships. (I figure a girl's got to stay current somehow, right?)

So there I was, browsing books on intimacy when one in particular caught my attention. I'd tell you the name of it, but that's the whole point. It didn't have a name. It was wrapped in red paper. Now that I think about it, it had probably been in a stack of similarly wrapped books on a table for Valentine's Day giving. In any case, there it was, red foil beckoning like the Sirens of Greek lore. I reached up to pluck it off the shelf.

The books were packed tighter than I thought. As I gave a tug on the volume in red, suddenly the entire shelf gave way. Books toppled everywhere. There was a loud crash as the shelf hit the floor, then an ongoing cascade of resounding smacks, bangs, and thumps as about fifty books followed suit.

The last book landed on the pile with a thick thud. A hush fell over the entire store. You could have heard a pin hit the floor. Suddenly a clerk behind the customer service counter shouted, "Are you okay?" and began sprinting toward me.

Was I *okay*? I wanted to say, "I'm standing ankle deep in sex manuals. Does it *look* like I'm okay?"

Instead, I started to laugh.

Russ came around the corner of the aisle. Shaking his head, he said, "How did I know it was going to be you?"

Ten minutes later when Linda returned to our table, Russ grinned. "Guess what you missed?"

Bless her heart, she tried to guess, but nothing she came up with was even close. When we finally told her the story, she laughed so hard I thought *she'd* be the one escorted off the premises instead of me.

Life may be about choices, but I'll tell you one thing for sure. Next time I'll make *my* choices in the cookbook aisle.

You choose, you lose

Sometimes, when we make a choice, we simply do the best we can with the information at hand. Door number one or number two? The job in Boise or the job in Duluth? Dinner at Denny's or lunch at Luigi's Lasagna Palace? The freeway looks slow this morning, would the side streets be quicker? Should I wear the brown pumps or the boots with fur at the cuff? Should I join the small group studying Galatians or the group staffing the soup kitchen? My son wants to play an instrument. Would he be more likely to practice the violin or tuba?

Sometimes we're happy with what we decide. Sometimes hindsight inspires us to draw a mental note to make a different choice next time. But something our decisions have in common is that, when there are two similar candidates, we really *do* try to make the best choice.

But every now and then a different kind of decision falls across our path. This choice isn't between two similar candidates at all. This choice is between a hundred dollar bill and, say, a rope burn. Or twenty sizzling ounces of hot-off-the-grill rib eye and, I don't know, a poisonous viper.

You would think such choices would be no-brainers. Instead, sometimes we need to have our heads examined.

Short-term relief?

A woman I know is thinking about renting a room in a house owned by someone she used to date. Not only does he own the house, he lives there and is currently dating other people. Less than a year ago, these two went through BTBU or Big Time Breakup. I mean, there were pieces of hearts everywhere. They still don't always get along that great. When I point out the certain heartache looming in her future, she nods her head in complete and total agreement and says, "I know. It's probably not the best idea, but I'm going to do it anyway."

Another woman I know is in the middle of a different set of discombobulating circumstances. She's so upset that she's been waking up in the middle of the night unable to sleep. She admitted, "I've been trying to figure out a way I can stop thinking about all my problems and get back to sleep. I mean, what am I supposed to do at 3:00 a.m.? I can't go the gym. I can't even call anyone. I don't know what to do with myself. So I've decided to have a drink when I can't sleep. It's the ideal solution. It'll help me stop worrying and even make me drowsy. It's perfect!"

Why do we do this? Why do we enthusiastically grab hold of things we *know* we're going to regret down the line? Not that I'm above doing the very same thing, because I'm not.

About ten years ago I was in a troubled marriage, the fact of which had not gone unnoticed by one of our acquaintances. All of a sudden he was dropping by the house during the day or calling me with offers to "be there for me" and "walk me through" this confusing and painful season in my life. And to be honest, the attention felt good, more than good. To quote Tony the Tiger, it felt *Grrrreat*! Somewhere inside, I knew that, if I let this friendship develop, I would be making a huge mistake— as in *Titanic* kind of huge. Still, he was *just* a friend, and it *would* be nice to have someone to talk to.

About that time a neighbor was flying into town and needed to be picked up at the airport—at five in the morning! At four, I threw on a pair of jeans and my most comfortable T-shirt—the oversized one with the slogan "Don't Go There" silk-screened on the front— ran a brush through my hair, and stumbled sleepily out the door. Forty-five minutes later, I was tossing my car keys on the conveyor belt and passing through the security checkpoint when a uniformed security guard asked, "What does that mean?"

I blinked. "What?" (Chitchat before 5:00 a.m. has never been my forte.)

"Your shirt. What does it mean?"

I looked down to see what I was wearing. "Nothing. It's just a shirt."

He was a Jamaican man, and I'll never forget the lilt of his voice as his eyes locked onto mine and he spoke these words from Proverbs 14:12: " 'There is a way that

seems right to a man, but in the end it leads to death.'
Don't go there."

And then, between the conveyor belt and the stream
of passengers moving me along, I suddenly found myself pushed on past the checkpoint and moving toward
the gates.

I looked back.

This is the part where I'd love to say he wasn't there
anymore, suggesting that he wasn't *actually* an immigrant
from Jamaica but was really an angel sent by God.

Nah, he was there. Inspecting someone's computer
bag, checking boarding passes, pointing a toddler-toting
mom in the direction of the bathrooms—just a guy doing
his job, tending to folks on their journeys, assisting them
with their baggage, and giving them a little direction
when they're in danger of losing their way.

Wait! Don't hurt me! Let *me* do it instead!

It's one thing to make the wrong choice by accident,
thinking it's your best option at the moment. It's something else altogether to make a choice you *know* in advance you're going to regret.

If you ask me, it's a form of self-sabotage, friendly
fire of the most personal kind. When you make this kind
of decision, you betray *you*. You take a bullet in the foot
and, guess what? When the police arrive, you're the one
holding the smoking gun.

I think you and I do this more than we realize. If we
really want to, say, pay off our credit cards, why in the

world do we go shopping and charge a bunch of new stuff? Likewise, if our goal is to lose thirty pounds, are we doing ourselves any favors by stocking the house with pecan praline ice cream and Butterfinger bars? (For the "kids," of course. *Wink, wink.*) And if we're truly serious about wanting the greatest marriage possible, do we *really* want to take this opportunity to forge a secret reconnection with that old flame on classmates.com?

If you and I *truly* want to experience peace, joy, and hope independent of our circumstances, what would happen if we stopped sabotaging ourselves by making the choices we *know* will complicate our lives, land us in troubled circumstances, and leave us feeling trapped, depressed, tormented, or even addicted?

Don't get me wrong. I'm not suggesting that you and I always make *pain-free* choices, but that we make *healthy* ones. Our goal is not to avoid *all* pain, because usually pain accompanies growth in our lives. We just want to avoid pain that's unnecessary and even counterproductive.

Sometimes a painful choice *is* the healthiest choice. When you stop ignoring the signs, admit your teenager may have a drug problem, and begin the sometimes-confrontational process of getting him the help he needs, that's not a painless decision, but it is a healthy one.

When you stop escaping the obvious, drag your spouse into counseling, and begin the hard work of forgiving hurts and learning from scratch how to love each other, that's not painless, but it's healthy.

Tackling that box of unopened mail, putting your phone back on the hook, contacting your creditors to see what you *really* owe, and making arrangements to get out of debt slowly but steadily, that's not painless, but it's healthy.

So a couple weeks ago, Skippy called.

Yes, yes, I know. You don't have to tell me it's insane. And you're right. I *don't* have to answer the phone. And I try not to, honestly. Sometimes I tell him not to call me. Sometimes I change his ring to "mute." I mean, I haven't even *seen* the guy in ten months. But every couple weeks he calls. Like clockwork. No, no, you're right. I've got boundary issues. I'm not disagreeing with you in the least.

Anyway, he called, and we started off doing exactly what we've been doing for months. He asks me about my life and inquires whether I'm seeing anyone and I tell him it's none of his business, and then he tells me about his life and I *never* ask if he's seeing anyone because, honestly, I *really* don't want to hear it. I think hearing it would break something for good. In me. Between us. All I know is that somewhere, somehow, something would definitely break for good.

So that's how everything started. And all the while I'm trying to protect myself from pain, trying to keep the conversation light and comfortable the way it *used* to feel, and wondering why I can't seem to move on.

Halfway through the phone call, it dawned on me that I'd been going about things the wrong way. Suddenly I knew *exactly* what I needed to do. Making my decision, I whispered a quick apology to my heart for the crushing blow that was about to come, braced myself, and asked him if there was anyone else in his life.

He said yes.

The rest of our conversation was brief and raw and honest. And I think maybe he'll stop calling now. And maybe that's okay. As far as choices go, the one I made wasn't painless, but it was healthy.

Choose life

What about you? Is there a choice in your life that you *know* is the healthy way to go?

There's a verse I love. It's Deuteronomy 30:19 and it goes like this: "I have set before you life and death, blessings and curses. Now choose life, so that you and your children may live."

But don't just read that one verse. You've gotta read the entire thirtieth chapter of the book of Deuteronomy. It's short, just twenty verses, but it's fascinating.

For the first eighteen verses, God warns the children of Israel that if they make certain choices, they will experience poverty, destruction, and even death. If they make different choices, they'll get prosperity and blessings and life. He goes into a lot of detail, talking about their enemies, their kids, and their livestock and crops. In the process he makes it all really clear. Make *this* choice, and you'll be blessed beyond your wildest dreams. Make *that* choice, and—to quote Mr. T—"we pity the fool!"

You'd think that would be enough right there. You'd think that, after saying all that, God wouldn't have had to come right out and add, "Now choose life." But he does. He says it just like that: "Now choose life."

And I guess I'm saying the same thing to you and me.

Do you want peace, joy, hope? Then choose life. Whether you're asking yourself what to eat for dinner tonight or how to handle midnight anxieties or where to live or what purchases to charge or whether an affair or substance abuse might work out well for you (despite the fact that they *never* work out well for anyone else) or whether a relationship you're in might benefit from intervention or counseling or just a hard dose of reality, see if one choice stands out from the rest as the healthiest option.

Sometimes we don't get a choice. Sometimes life hands us stuff we didn't choose, didn't want, wish desperately we could return.

So when there *are* choices to make—especially if we're choosing between a rib eye and a viper—let's try to remember that *some* pain is unnecessary. Who wants it? Who needs it? So don't go there.

I wish I always made the right choices. Unfortunately, I make the same mistakes you do. Maybe even more. But that's how we know how to love each other and lift each other up and encourage each other always toward the highest and healthiest path. And even when we goof and choose the stuff we know will bring us pain (and we *all* do it now and then), let's forgive each other, forgive ourselves, and learn from those mistakes.

This is exactly why, the next time you run into me at Barnes and Noble, I'll be sitting quietly, keeping my hands to myself and reading a cookbook.

Turn on a Light

- Have you ever known ahead of time that a choice was the wrong one but you made it anyway? Why did you make the choice you did? How did it turn out for you?

- Think of a time you made a healthy choice even though it was hard. How did you find the inner strength to make that painful or difficult choice?

- Have you ever regretted making a choice you knew was right?

- When your circumstances seem dim and you feel desperate for a little light, you may be tempted to make choices that promise temporary relief in exchange for more pain down the road. Name some choices that could fall into this category. What alternatives might you have?

8

You Can't Always Believe
Your Own Eyes

Our final dress rehearsal was a fiasco. Nothing went right. At any moment I expected to see Larry, Moe, and Curly chase each other across the stage.

It was ten o'clock on the Saturday night before the big Easter production, and we were in trouble.

The actors and actresses had their parts beautifully memorized. All the costumes looked authentic. The special-effects makeup—for the demons, the harlots of hell, Satan, and even Jesus during the scene when he is whipped by a Roman soldier—was gripping and vivid. The fog machine was fogging beautifully. Even the two chickens and the lamb were psyched and excited for their cameos.

The problem—and it was a doozy—had to do with the sets.

We had amazing sets—huge backdrops, a rolling tomb, a moveable forest, a pillared balcony from which Pilate could address the restless crowd, and a marketplace filled with the carts of gregarious merchants. Plus we had clay pots, bales of hay, a crate of chickens, and that lamb I mentioned. There was even a modern-day bedroom complete with a full-sized bed.

In other words, there was a lot of stuff—big stuff—moving off and on that stage between each of our twelve scenes. And we weren't using curtains. (I say *we* because it was my job—along with five stagehands—to make sure the transitions went smoothly.) Between scenes, the lights simply went dark, and my crew and I had roughly two minutes to dart onto the shadowy stage and perform our magic, moving trees and boulders and beds and chickens while the soundtrack played.

Unfortunately, the dinner theater our church had rented for Easter services had been unavailable for rehearsals until our final dress rehearsal one night before Easter Sunday. In the meantime, we'd been practicing on a makeshift stage in our director's backyard. And while everything had gone smoothly on our backyard stage, transitioning to the *real* stage was turning out to be another story. Half-filled with set pieces from prior productions, the dinner theater stage offered us a lot less space than we'd envisioned. Not only did we keep bumping into each other while carrying boulders and trees, there always seemed to be something from the previous scene standing in the way of something we needed for the scene coming up.

Around eleven that night, rehearsal ended and we let the cast go home. To say everyone was discouraged was an understatement. As the last of us locked up and headed to our cars, I turned to Doug Staller, the director, and said, "I'll go home and see if I can come up with some sort of chart that might—"

"Karen," he said as gently as he could. "It's too late. I think we should all do the best we can in the morning, and in the afternoon catch the first plane out of the country."

"But if I made some sort of a list . . ."

I knew how much trouble we were in when this can-do sort of guy shook his head and said, "Go home. Go to bed. We're past the point of paper. Right now, the most important thing is sleep. We'll get through it somehow."

"Past the point of paper?" I blinked in disbelief. "Are you kidding me? Writers are *never* past the point of paper."

I worked all night. At six the next morning, I was at Kinko's making color copies. By seven I was at the theater, dividing my crew into teams and handing out stapled booklets filled with diagrams of the stage during all twelve scene transitions. I had color-coded and choreographed the precise steps of every team and every set piece or prop coming or going.

There was no time to rehearse. We went immediately into our first performance. A second performance followed later that morning.

You can see photos of these performances by going to www.poweruproductions.org. But let me just say that, on stage, a talented cast of forty men, women, and children (and several farm animals) performed beautifully. Backstage, my crew performed beautifully as well. Stage transitions were seamless. Every boulder, tree, bed, animal, balcony, and clay pot came and went like clockwork.

That morning several thousand people sitting in the audience watched an amazing story unfold before their eyes. But like two sides of the same coin—or perhaps I should say like two sides of the same curtain—backstage there had been another story, another set of performers, another dance the audience never got to see.

More than meets the eye

I still enjoy the memories of that adventure. The images are so vivid it feels like yesterday instead of four years ago. In fact, now that I think about it, it's been four years almost to the day. I say this because, as I write these words, it's late April and we celebrated Easter just last week.

Not that it *feels* like spring. This very moment I'm looking out my window at my front deck buried in eight inches of fresh snow. The pine trees in my front yard look weary, their limbs hanging low to the ground, heavy with snow and ice.

No, it definitely doesn't feel like spring, although living in Colorado Springs, I should probably start going by the calendar instead of by a thermometer. Sometimes it even snows here in June. The weather here is always an E-ticket ride (and if you're too young to know what that means, ask someone over thirty-five).

How weird is the weather here? An hour ago I spoke with Kaitlyn. She's forty-five minutes away in Denver, in a dorm room at Colorado Christian University. She says it's raining there, but there's no sign of snow and it's not even cold. And to make matters even more surreal, this morning I got an email from my sisters. They're vacationing in Argentina, where they say it's green and lush and warm.

But here it's snowing and snowing and snowing. With predictions of a whiteout, they canceled school today, which is why my daughter Kacie and my nephews Hunter and Isaac are running around unrestrained in my home.

So far they've played video games, trained Buddy the dog to perform for Cheese Puffs, logged on to www. youtube.com, and watched themselves in videos masterminded by my other nephew Connor (go to www.you tube.com, search connor berge, and watch "The Cookie Caper"). They've gorged themselves on bagels, ham sandwiches, Fruity Pebbles, and "ice cream" made out of snow and half-and-half. Not that I've had to witness any of this. I've been holed up in my room, writing, but I've been getting occasional reports. And the one time I ventured into my disheveled kitchen, I could see that, yep, everything they'd told me was true.

And since apparently this chapter has digressed into some sort of report on my day, I might as well tell you about something else memorable that happened.

Several hours ago, Kacie handed me a package that arrived in yesterday's mail. She explained that last week she'd gone onto eBay, found something she knew I'd like, then used my Paypal account to buy it. She told me it was a present from her, then handed me $6.46 to reimburse me for the gift.

I tore open the package and gasped.

I was holding a little paperback book by Eleanor Cameron titled, *The Wonderful Flight to the Mushroom Planet*. When I was a kid, I must have checked this book out of my elementary school library a dozen times. I *loved* this little book and had mentioned it several times to my kids. And now, nearly four decades later, I have my own copy, courtesy of Kacie, who apparently has the memory of an elephant.

I hollered, "Story time!" and before I knew it, Isaac, Kacie, and Hunter had latched onto the idea and taken it further than I'd ever imagined. Deciding I needed to look "grandmotherish," Kacie tried to talk me into wearing fuzzy slippers and drawing wrinkles on my face. I held my ground with a counter offer, saying, "I'm not letting you anywhere near my face with that permanent marker, but I *will* concede to the sequined reading glasses." The kids, getting in touch with their inner kindergarten, grabbed "blankies," graham crackers, and stuffed animals, plopped themselves on the floor in front of me and were all antsy with anticipation. Or maybe they were pretending to be antsy with anticipation. Although I'm hoping they were only *pretending* to pretend, because you should never be too old for story time, even if you *are* nine, twelve, and thirteen.

105

So it was very cool. They got six chapters out of me, plus a promise to read the rest aloud later.

So now they're bouncing around in the other room, and after all that distraction, I'm finally back to writing, occasionally looking out at the snow and thinking about that Easter drama four years ago and how everything that happened backstage was just as real as everything that happened in the spotlight, even if the audience couldn't see a thing we were doing back there.

I'm also thinking how interesting it is that, in the world beyond my little snow-filled yard, it can be raining for Kaitlyn and tropical for my sisters. And how, even though my eyes and feelings are shouting "winter!" it can *actually* be springtime. And how a woman can be sitting blissfully unaware in her bedroom while three kids can be trashing an entire kitchen.

And how—as we're trudging along, convinced our lives are predictable and boring and that nothing will ever change—someone can be working secretly on our behalf, thinking of our fondest desires, finding gifts to make us laugh with delight, and making elaborate plans to surprise us by sending those good things our way.

Now you see it. Now you don't. Or is it the other way around?

Even the Bible tells us there's stuff we don't see, stuff that's real but that—at least for a season—exists in a place and time we can't see from where we happen to be standing.

First Corinthians 13:9–12 reminds us that everything we know is only part of the picture, that our perspective changes as we grow and mature, and that today we're looking into a dim mirror but one day our vision will be unfettered.

In Jeremiah 29:11 God says to a group of people suffering in exile, "Look, I realize you can't see it or feel it at the moment, but I know what I've got in store for you, and I've got plans to bless you rather than harm you, plans to give you hope and a future" (my paraphrase).

And in Hebrews once again we're reminded that good things exist beyond the scope of what we currently possess or see. The exact words go like this: "Now faith is the substance of things hoped for, the evidence of things not seen" (Heb. 11:1 KJV). *Substance*. I like that word. To me, *substance* means something is "there." It exists. In other words, faith is the existence of things we don't have and can't see—at least not *yet*.

I'm a pretty visual person. If something is out of sight for me, it ceases to exist. This is why I'm a horrible long-distance friend. This is why I can't use file folders and I often abandon handbags and carry my wallet, keys, cell phone, and sunglasses around in my hands. Yes, it's unwieldy, but at least I don't have to keep checking the bowels of my purse every five minutes to make sure the essentials I dropped in there still exist.

But even more than trying to limit reality to what I see, I'm guilty of trying to limit it to how I *feel*. Maybe it's because I'm a woman, and women are said to be more influenced by emotions than are men, who tend to be more visual. But whatever the reason, all I know is that it's *way* too easy for me to forget that things—good things—exist even when my emotions try to convince me otherwise.

Meanwhile, back at the ranch . . .

How much do you and I want to free our emotions from the tyranny of our circumstances? We'll never be able to do it until we know what it means to believe—*really* believe—in the existence of stuff we can't see or feel.

The truth is, our circumstances as we see them, and even our emotions at any given moment, are just a piece of the puzzle . . .

- a dieter's sliver of a twelve-layer wedding cake
- a tiny peephole overlooking the smallest corner of a sweeping landscape
- a lone spotlight illuminating a modest circle on an otherwise dark stage stretching a hundred feet from end to end
- a thirty-second clip culled from a three-hour movie
- a three-foot-square picnic blanket smack dab in the middle of a football field.

In other words, beyond the periphery of what we are experiencing at any given moment with our eyes and with our heart, there's more, a lot more, more of everything. What kind of everything? You name it: opportunities, gifts, second chances, surprises, answers, rescue, laughter, courage, love, good intentions, good people, peace, happiness, and joy. Not to mention other stuff we can't necessarily see or touch, like the laws of gravity, the healing properties of time, and even God himself. These things aren't pretend. Maybe we can't *see* them right now. Maybe we don't *feel* like they exist, but that doesn't change the fact that they're out there.

I don't know about you but I don't *want* to know everything. I like the fact that, two months or two minutes from now, anything can happen. And I couldn't be happier that what I feel at any given moment isn't the whole story, but a single frame in an epic four-reel movie. I love knowing that just because I *feel* hopeless doesn't *actually* mean there's no hope, and, at the very moment I'm feeling fearful, numb, or trapped, that safety, joy, and progress are actually waiting in the wings, listening for their cue to step into the spotlight.

So what now?

Can understanding all this stuff *really* aid us in our quest to free our emotions from the tyranny of our circumstances and enable us to hang on to peace, joy, and hope even when we are having a really bad day? Can this understanding help us have a fabulous, happy life when our circumstances look dim?

You bet it can. The truth is, when we use this knowledge in the right way, it's kind of like credit, letting us take something that's coming our way *tomorrow* and enjoying the benefits of that thing *today*. Or like a cash advance on a paycheck that has yet to arrive in the mail. Except there's no interest, and the good feelings we borrow from the future never have to be returned.

Indeed, faith is the best way I know to enjoy a little bit of tomorrow's blessings before the sun goes down today.

So how can we exercise that faith, reaching into the future and borrowing a smile from tomorrow? Let's find out.

Believing *is* seeing

I'm writing these words on Monday, knowing that Thursday—just a few days from now—Kaitlyn comes home from college. Okay, not for good but for the summer, and for the mom who misses her, that's good enough.

The moment she walks in my front door, I'm going to break into a Cheshire-cat grin. Merely anticipating her arrival in three days puts a smile on my face today. She may not be here yet, but knowing she's on her way means I can, this very afternoon, enjoy a taste of the smorgasbord of happy emotions I know I'll experience in the near future when I hear her car engine in my driveway.

By picturing an event I'm confident will occur in the near future, I can let myself begin to experience some of the emotions I know I'll feel then.

I heard a story several months ago that really hit home. In a war-torn country, a Christian pastor was captured by armed guerillas, handed a shovel, and ordered to dig his own grave. The leader of the gang waved a machine gun at the captive and told him that, as soon as the shallow grave was finished, he would be shot. That pastor began to dig, and his strokes were—as you can well imagine!—lethargic and unenthusiastic. Almost in a daze, the pastor said resignedly to himself, *I guess this is it. I guess I'm going home.* Soon he began shoveling faster and harder. As the gang members watched in disbelief, the pastor shoveled even faster, looking almost happy now despite the perspiration coating his face. He was still talking, repeating a single phrase over and over and with greater enthusiasm every minute when one of his captors stopped him and said, "Speak up! Are you crazy? What are you saying?" The pastor, beaming beneath a layer of sweat and grime, grinned and said, "I'm going home. I'm actually going *home!*"

Befuddled, the guerillas turned the *loco* pastor loose but not before he had a chance to tell them how it was he'd been able to look beyond the stuff he *could* see—like that half-dug grave—and borrow his crazy joy from things he had yet to see, like a Savior named Jesus and a home called heaven.

There's a church hymn that ends with the line, "I've got faith like a river in my soul." I love that image.

Think of everything a river does. It makes things grow. It can move you from one place to another. It hydrates and refreshes. It makes you buoyant. A river is even filled with food. And on a clear, sunny day, walk to the stretch of river where quiet waters run deep, look at the glassy surface, and you'll see nothing but blue sky.

Believing in good stuff we can't see yet—opportunities, second chances, rescue, surprises, and even a loving and personal God—has many of the same benefits. This belief will help you grow. It brings progress. Faith can move you from one place to another, financially, emotionally, spiritually, physically, geographically, and any other way you can imagine. Faith brings healing and refreshment. Faith makes you buoyant and lifts your spirit. Faith is nourishing to the soul. And where faith runs deep and peace prevails, there's a very good chance that, if you know just how to look, you can catch a glimpse of heaven reflected there.

Our emotions are not the be-all and end-all. They don't define reality. Sometimes they don't even reflect reality. And every now and then our emotions are so out of touch with reality, they don't even exchange Christmas cards once a year.

If you ask me, that's good news, because it means we don't *have* to let our circumstances dictate our emotions, or our emotions define the world as we see it. It also means we can start drawing joy, peace, and hope from a greater realm beyond what we may be presently seeing or experiencing in our lives.

Of course, I know all too well that when you or I get busy or distracted, it's easy to forget all this, so I'm thinking we should keep something around to help us remember, something that, whenever we see it, reminds us that there's a good God with good plans, that surprises are waiting in the wings, and that the cliché "Seeing is believing" may be truest when reversed.

I know what will remind me, and I think I'll go out this afternoon and find some. I'll even put some in the mail to you so you can be reminded too.

Does anyone know how to mail a couple of chickens and a lamb?

Turn on a Light

- Can you believe good things are coming your way even when your eyes and heart are telling you otherwise?

- What does the word *faith* mean to you? Does it apply to anything I've written about in this chapter?

- Do you believe in a personal God who has a plan for your life and wants to send good things your way? Why or why not?

9

Help! I'm Talking
and I Can't Shut Up

One day I picked up the phone and called one of my sisters. I started off by saying, "Hi! It's me . . . ," talked for fifteen minutes, and hung up the phone. About that time one of my daughters asked, "So how's she doing?"

I blinked. "Who?"

"Aunt Shelly."

"How would I know? That was her answering machine."

Another friend, Kathy, told me that when she gets home from work, listens to her voicemail, and starts to hear my voice, she makes herself a cup of coffee and pulls up a chair because she knows it'll be a long message and she might as well be comfortable. "Besides," she says, "this way it's like we've just had a nice long chat over coffee." (Technical question: Does "chat over coffee" apply if one person does all the talking and the other one gets all the coffee?)

I figure this tells us two things. The first is that I like to talk. The second is that listeners are optional.

But I knew it was *really* bad when comedians in my town started opening their acts by saying, "If Karen Linamen started talking in the woods and there was no one around to hear her, would local weather stations still register fluctuations in air pressure?"

All this talking has benefits. For example, my winter heating bills are probably lower than yours. Plus I can open pickle jars with my jaws. And how many people do you know who have gotten phone solicitors to hang up on *them*?

I guess another benefit to talking is the whole venting thing. Sometimes you just feel better after mouthing off. Whether it's twenty minutes of whining or a full-fledged rant, there's not a one of us who doesn't know what it feels like to release pent-up steam via a flapping jaw.

Finally, talking goes great with pretty much any other activity. I don't know if it's because I'm a woman or what, but I'm great at multitasking. I can do almost anything while talking. I can drink coffee and talk. I can wash dishes and talk. I can paint my nails, drive a car, watch a movie, or even read a book while maintaining a steady monologue. The one thing I can't do yet is talk while applying lip liner. But I'm practicing.

Talking up a storm?

A few minutes ago Kacie looked over my shoulder and started reading the exact paragraphs you just read. After a moment she looked at me and said, "Wow. Do comedians here in town really talk about you?"

"Well, no. That's just a joke."

She read a few more lines, then said, "Can you really do that? Open pickle jars with your mouth?"

"Actually, I think that would probably break my teeth. I'm exaggerating. You know, hyperbole." (She's been studying *hyperbole* in her sixth grade English class.)

She grinned. "Got it."

I really am a verbal person. I'm so verbal that someone who lives with me thinks eventually my name *could* show up in David Letterman's monologue, and that I really *have* developed my jaw muscles to the point of performing impressive shows of force against noncompliant food storage devices. And my phone messages to Michelle and Kathy really did happen, exactly like I said. So I wasn't joking about those.

And I *definitely* wasn't joking about venting.

My guess is that you do the same thing. When circumstances send our emotions careening wildly in any direction, sometimes we've just gotta talk about it. The need to describe, debrief, process, analyze, solve, or vent can be enormous. When I need to talk, I've bent the ears of friends, parents, my husband, random cashiers and clerks, therapists, God, and even my German shepherd, Walter. (I've never sought advice from my Boston terrier. I don't know why. Now that

I think about it, this might be something to talk about with my therapist.)

Sometimes the point of talking is to, you know, just talk. Woe to the husband who listens to his wife for thirty seconds and then actually *attempts to solve* whatever problem has gotten her so upset. Such husbands would be my biggest supporters if I ever wanted to sell T-shirts to women that said, "Don't make me stop talking about my problems to listen to your perfectly viable solutions— I'm running out of places to hide the bodies." Eventually my husband learned to ask, "So, is this something you want me to actually *solve*, or do you just want me to listen and look sympathetic?" Unfortunately, he only learned to ask this after a number of near-death experiences and several surface wounds.

So, yeah, when we're troubled, we talk. And occasionally all that venting is just what the doctor ordered. But sometimes all that outflow of energy can keep us from receiving whatever it is we *really* need at that moment. And this makes me think of drowning.

I've never been a lifeguard. While saving lives is admirable, I'm of the opinion that the best way I can serve humanity is by avoiding swimsuits and staying fully clothed. But I *know* a lifeguard. Wondering if all that thrashing around makes it harder to rescue someone, I asked Jess if she's ever had to knock anyone unconscious to save their life. She said she hasn't—yet—but that it's something lifeguards have to be prepared to do. She said that "active rescues," the kind performed on thrashing folks, are a lot harder and require different techniques than "passive rescues" performed on folks who *aren't* thrashing.

I think the whole thrashing thing is a good image of what can happen when we over-vent. Are our tongues thrashing when they should be resting? Do we prattle on when tuning in might serve us better? Are we trying to elucidate instead of listen? Sure, we're panicked but, if you ask me, all that outgoing verbal energy can hinder us from receiving the incoming help or wisdom we so desperately need.

In these moments, we would be wise to remember the words of that celebrated hunter and savvy philosopher Elmer Fudd and do exactly as he advises: "Shhhh. Be quiet. Be vewy vewy quiet."

La-la-la. I can't hear you. La-la-la.

I had something like this happen to me several years ago. The whole thing started one Thursday night. Finding myself divorced and single for the first time in twenty-some years, I decided to check out a Christian online dating site.

I logged on and, sure enough, in no time at all I was exchanging instant messages with a nice man who lived in North Carolina. Half an hour later he suggested I call him on the phone, and I agreed despite the lateness of the hour. Toward the end of a very pleasant and uplifting conversation, he got a little flirtatious, then suggestive. Ignoring the alarms going off in my head, I let the conversation travel farther than I knew was right or prudent.

Shortly it took another turn as his comments crossed even *that* border and started heading toward scaryland. I ended the phone call.

The next morning I reflected on our conversation and winced. I prayed right then, asking God to forgive me for . . . well, to be honest, enjoying the conversation as long as I did. Then I thanked him for forgiving me. I also made the decision to avoid certain situations in the future. For instance, I wasn't going to lower my guard so fast with strangers. And late night phone calls were an obvious invitation for a premature sense of intimacy. I would definitely be more careful. Besides, there was the safety factor. I could have been talking to anybody, like a serial killer, or worse, a serial killer with caller ID.

That's when I panicked.

I wasn't worried about my soul. I had made a mistake, repented, been forgiven, and learned something in the process. Such is the nature of life—even the Christian life—and anyone who says differently should consider a career writing fiction.

No, suddenly I was worried about safety. I'd naively called this guy on my home line. What if he *did* have caller ID? What if he started calling my house? What if he showed up at my front *door*? I felt like a sheep who had wandered away from the fold and gotten cozy with a wolf. I started praying again, but this time I was panicked and rambling. For fifteen minutes I spilled my anxieties out to God, begging for protection, venting my fears, berating myself for being naive and stupid. And on top of everything else, I was haunted by *this* thought:

What if anyone found out about this? How humiliating would *that* be?

For all my nonstop talking, I suddenly felt as though my words were going as far as the ceiling and bouncing back. Was God listening?

Was I?

I was living near Denver and attending Jubilee Fellowship Church at the time, and Pastor John had preached on this very subject a few weeks earlier. In fact, he'd been pretty blunt about it. He'd said that sometimes the secret to hearing God is shutting your mouth. So I took a deep breath and closed my mouth.

At first, I think I did more *thinking about listening* than actual listening, because my brain kept spinning with things like, "Okay, God, I'm listening. I really need to hear something from you. Are you there? Can't you tell me what to do? Are you saying anything to me? Wait . . . is that your voice? Are you saying everything will be okay? No . . . hold on . . . is *that* your voice? Are you telling me I messed up and now I'll have to deal with it? Hello? Are you there? Because I'm listening, Lord. No, really. I mean it this time. For real . . ."

I was swallowing water, begging for rescue, but thrashing so wildly even a Navy Seal would have had a hard time approaching me.

About that time, something began to dawn on me. It was a growing awareness of something that had been there for some time. You may have had the same feeling. You know, the one you get when you're coming out of a deep sleep and the beeping of your alarm clock starts to penetrate your foggy brain and you realize you've been hearing that annoying noise for a while but it wasn't sinking in until now. Well, it was just like that.

Except it wasn't a sound. It was an image.

I had a picture in my head and, as I became aware of it, I realized it had been there for some time, quietly flashing in the background like some subtle strobe. I just hadn't been paying attention. The image was of me, sitting in the office of my pastor.

At that moment I was flooded with peace.

Over the next hour, I became increasingly certain of what I needed to do. My fears were gone. I felt peaceful and safe. I remember spending the morning humming happily, feeling ever so grateful to my heavenly Father for answering my prayer. I really was in awe over the whole thing. God had not only listened to my cry for help, he had given me a solution. But it would have gone unnoticed if I hadn't closed my mouth and calmed my spirit enough to hear it—or, as it turned out, see it!

I called the church office. Pastor John said he could see me first thing Tuesday morning, which was pretty good considering it was already noon on Friday and he would be out of the office on Monday. Then I called a couple of my closest friends. Finally, I emailed Mr. North Carolina. I wished him well and asked him not to contact me in the future. I told him I'd goofed up, and that our conversation didn't represent who I was or wanted to be. I told him I'd not only spoken to my pastor, but had explained everything to a couple friends of mine, giving them permission to ask me about future conversations and to encourage me to a higher standard of behavior.

After hitting "send," I logged off my computer. Wow. Two hours ago I'd been afraid of two things: embarrassing secrets and becoming a target, like that lone sheep I talked about. Suddenly I *had* no secrets, and I wasn't isolated anymore. Even Mr. North Carolina knew I wasn't easy pickins. My emotions had gone from nuclear panic to peace and gratitude.

Receiving lane

There are no two ways around it. Sometimes we just need to shut up and listen. Indeed, if we listened more, how might our lives be different?

A marriage counselor told me, "People pay me a hundred dollars an hour to tell them what their spouse has been telling them all along for free."

I met a woman who told me she had struggled for years with negative thinking and a poor self-image. When I suggested a tape series on this very subject, she brushed aside my recommendation, saying, "Those things are worthless. If you ask me, the only people being helped by self-help tapes are the people selling the tapes and getting rich." And then she went on complaining.

Begging God for answers and direction, we drone and ramble so much that sometimes he has a hard time getting a word in edgewise.

I've struggled with procrastination for years. (This makes sense. What procrastinator realizes she has a problem and then solves it immediately?) But I found a book—*Eat That Frog* by Brian Tracy—that may help. I've scanned several chapters but have yet to read the whole thing and apply the principles. (I'll get around to it. No, really!) But my point is, there are books out there that can actually help me avoid the unpleasant feelings and ramifications that come from spending my life running behind. That's the good news. The bad news is that I have to stop running long enough to sit still and *read* them.

This whole subject reminds me of a cartoon I saw a long time ago. All around a tent, armies in primitive armor are fighting each other with swords and spears. Inside the tent a frazzled warlord is saying to his second-in-command, "Salesperson? Can't you see we're losing this battle? I don't have *time* to listen to a salesperson right now!" And just outside the tent, a salesman waits in vain, cradling the product he had hoped to hawk—a machine gun.

There's all sorts of good stuff out there that can help us change the circumstances that are making us crazy, or at least help us manage the crazies if we can't change the circumstances. That is, *if* we're willing to stop what we're doing, take a deep breath, and listen.

What kind of good stuff?

When we listen, we can receive information, exhortation, encouragement, and advice. We can welcome wise counsel. We can benefit from examples, role models, and mentoring. We might be handed game plans, strategies, suggestions, and solutions. We can receive comfort or straight talk.

But none of these things can make a smattering of difference in our life until we settle down, open our ears and maybe even our heart, and put ourselves in an attitude to receive.

After all, whining might get us attention, but listening can get us results.

I hear ya. Now what?

Getting back to my story . . .

On Thursday I'd made a mistake. On Friday morning I panicked until I stopped thrashing long enough to receive the rescue I needed. When I stopped thrashing, God gave me an answer to my dilemma, and I experienced tremendous peace as a result.

By the time Tuesday rolled around, I was feeling pretty good about things. After all, my problem had been solved. Was this final step necessary? Did I *really* need to meet with my pastor? I toyed with the idea of calling Pastor John and canceling our appointment. Then I shook the idea out of my head and went to find my car keys.

After all, it's important to quiet yourself long enough to receive good advice or wise counsel, but if you just *hear* it and don't actually *do* it, how can you get the full benefit?

I didn't want to shortchange myself. I also wanted to be obedient. Even though it *felt* like my problem had been solved, I knew it was important for me to follow through with what God had told me to do when I'd cried out to him.

Pastor John and I had a great time together. We talked; we prayed. I left his office feeling encouraged and inspired.

I had *stopped* thrashing.

I had *listened*.

I'd *received* wise counsel.

I'd *acted* on that wise counsel.

It worked out well for me. I'm sure you've had times when you've done the same thing and it's worked out well for you too. If only we could remember to follow this pattern more often!

For what it's worth, we're not the *only* ones on the face of the planet who have to be reminded to stop and listen. It's an age-old problem. If it weren't, David would never have written the words that can be found in the forty-sixth psalm. Actually he wrote these words as lyrics to a song. As I read them, I can't imagine what the melody would sound like, but I know that the words strike a chord in my own soul.

In about ten verses of this psalm, David describes *really* unpleasant circumstances—earthquakes, tidal waves, international uproar, war, and destruction. (Wow! After that list, *my* life is looking better all the time!)

So why isn't he afraid even when he's in the middle of stuff that's really scary? He writes, "God is our refuge and strength, an ever-present help in trouble. Therefore we will not fear, though the earth give way and the mountains fall into the heart of the sea, though its waters roar and foam and the mountains quake with their surging" (vv. 1–3).

And then he gives a directive from God. It's simply this: "Be still, and know that I am God" (v. 10).

There's other stuff in there, but it's all stuff that God gets to do, like ending wars and being a fortress and helping and giving us strength. Sometimes, *our* primary job during scary stuff is to be still.

I wish the scary stuff didn't happen or the sad stuff or even the stupid stuff we manage to get ourselves into. But when it does, sometimes the best thing we can do is stop thrashing, sit still, and listen—to our own conscience, to our spouse, to a good tape series, to parents, to nature, to God, to a wise friend, even to an episode of Mayberry R.F.D. Because when we're in receiving mode, it's amazing where we can find nuggets of wisdom. My kids, an airport security guard, even SpongeBob SquarePants have unknowingly said things to me that—when I really listened—rang true with something I'd known all along but wouldn't admit to myself, or it shed new light on something I'd been wrestling with.

We can go to libraries or churches, classrooms or counselors. Nature can be a wise teacher. The psalmist wrote in Psalm 121 that when he needed help, he lifted his eyes to the hills. Norm Wright apparently looks a little lower, judging from the title of his book *The Perfect Catch: Lessons for Life from a Bass Fisherman.* And who hasn't taken a reflective walk in the woods only to come away with some principle, insight, or inspiration to apply to life?

But we can't benefit from any of it unless we know how to close our mouths and open our ears.

King David and Elmer Fudd knew what they were talking about after all.

Turn on a Light

- When your circumstances look dim and you need some answers, do you vent? Do you listen? Do you vent *then* listen?

- What are some signs that it might be time to stop whining and start listening?

- Not all advice is good advice. Are you convinced that what you're hearing is right and wise? How can you know?

- When you need to hear from God, what do you do? How do you put yourself in a frame of mind, heart, and spirit to listen—really listen—to what he might be saying to you? How do you get all the white noise in your head to calm down so that the still, small voice of your Creator doesn't get lost in the static?

- At a silent retreat, participants take a temporary vow of silence. For several hours or several days, they close their mouths and turn down the volume of the noise of the world. *Ahhh . . . that's better.* Suddenly they can actually hear themselves think. Maybe even hear God speak. This week arrange your own mini silent retreat. Set aside a predetermined amount of time (two hours, four hours, an entire day—the length is up to you). Turn off the cell phone. Turn off the TV. Turn off the iPod. Turn off the dialogue with family, friends, or strangers. Take a walk. Listen to your footsteps. Listen to God. Just listen.

10

Whenever I Feel Blue, I Start Breathing Again

A few nights ago Kaitlyn and I found ourselves at Famous Footwear during their buy-one-pair-get-another-pair-half-price sale. While looking for neutral summer sandals, Kaitlyn discovered several very *non*-neutral pairs of shoes that she loved. One was navy with white polka dots. The other was an animal print pump perfect for fall or winter wear.

With a wince, Kaitlyn put the shoes back on the rack.

"What are you doing?" I asked.

She said, "I *want* these shoes, but I don't really *need* them."

I know. I couldn't believe it either. I mean, as a mother you try and try to raise your kids right, and then they go and pull something like this. All I can say is that she didn't get this kind of attitude from me.

I sighed. "If I've told you once, I've told you a thousand times. Shoes are not a *want*. A Rolex watch is a want. Vegetables are a want. Even housecleaning is optional. New shoes are a *need*."

Apparently my little lecture backfired on me.

At the checkout counter, I hesitated over a pair of leather boots I'd picked out. One of the things these boots had going for them was the fact that they brought our total shoe purchase to four pairs of shoes, meaning I could buy the boots at half price. But with a similar pair of brown boots at home, would I really wear them? Decisions, decisions.

Sensing my quandary, my sensible daughter said, "Don't get the boots."

I sighed. "Yeah, you're right."

"Because if you *don't* get them, I can get this amazing pair of lime green skimmers that I fell in love with!" And with that, she raced back into the aisles to claim the green skimmers.

Maslow *meant* to mention shoes

There are just certain things you and I *have* to have if we're going to feel and function at our best. New shoes are at the top of the list.

Next comes air.

Then chocolate.

Then sleep.

Then food and water.

Abraham Maslow organized our basic needs another way. According to him, our most urgent primary needs are physiological, meaning the things we have to have just to stay alive. This category includes air, food, water, and sleep.

Once these needs are met, we're free to start thinking about things like health, shelter, and where our next paycheck is coming from. When we feel safe and secure, our need for love and belonging takes center stage and we crave friendship, sexual intimacy, and family bonds. Next come esteem needs, our longing for confidence, success, and respect.

Last but not least, you and I have a need to fulfill our potential as human beings. Maslow puts our longing for morality, creativity, spontaneity, and problem-solving in this category.

I don't know where Maslow intended to put our need for new shoes. I'm sure it belongs in there somewhere.

The point is that you and I have basic needs. And when those needs go unmet, our emotions can nose-dive. If you don't believe me, think about how, when you're tired or hungry, small annoyances can feel so much more exaggerated or traumatic. For instance, you know that insensitive thing your husband did? For his sake, let's hope he didn't spring it on you when you were functioning on two hours' sleep after being up all night with flu-riddled kids! No matter *what's* going on in our lives at any given moment, it's all going to *feel* a lot worse when we're tired or hungry. When our basic needs for things like oxygen, water, food, or sleep are going unmet, we can have a hard time mustering feelings of peace, happiness, and hope even in the *best* of circumstances!

Back to basics

I'm convinced there's a basic need that didn't make it onto Maslow's list (I mean besides the shoe thing). And as long as this particular need goes unmet, you and I can't function at our best. We crave this thing, even though sometimes we don't even realize it.

I'll tell you what this basic need is in a minute. But first, let me say that I thought a lot about cravings when I was writing my last book, *Chocolatherapy: Satisfying the Deepest Cravings of Your Inner Chick*. And something that struck me as fascinating is how often we *think* we're craving one thing when we're *really* longing for something else altogether.

For example, one day I was incredibly stressed. My new cell phone wasn't working, my laptop had crashed, and my renters were behind on their rent. So naturally I made a beeline for the cake and ice cream. Actually, *first* I found an eight-by-eight-inch Pyrex dish. *Then* I made a beeline for the cake and ice cream. What I have discovered is that you can fit four pieces of cake nicely in the bottom of an eight-by-eight-inch dish. Top it off with a third of a carton of ice cream and you're definitely on your way to a sweet little sugar buzz and then a nice long nap.

At some point while preparing my drug of choice, I realized the lethargy and nap that would follow my sugar high was what I was *really* after. But even this wasn't what I really *really* needed. At that moment I had a true, legitimate need. I needed a breather, a temporary reprieve from my stress so I could regroup and think clearly how to solve my problems. But I wasn't fully aware of what my legitimate need was. I *thought* I needed the numbing escape that would come from overdoing on cake.

In a similar way, there's something you and I crave. It's something really basic that we need to function at our best. Unfortunately, we're not always *aware* that we need this thing. Sometimes we get confused and think we need other things instead. But that doesn't change the fact that this need is real, it's urgent, and it's been hardwired into our very core from before the beginning of time.

It all started in a garden.

Before taking their first breath of air, their first long drink of spring water, or their first bite of organically grown garden fare, a man and woman were created by God, in the image of God, for God. They were created to be in his presence, hang out with him, love him, talk with him, walk with him.

This was the reason for their existence.

I don't know exactly when Adam and Eve grew conscious of the extent of their need for fellowship with God but I know that the need was there. After all, it was kneaded into their very beings by the hands of the God who crafted their bodies from clay. It was breathed into their nostrils by the Deity who desired their company. Whether they realized it or not, Adam and Eve *needed* to spend time in the presence of God.

And so do we.

Just your garden-variety invitation

Once a month I attend a nondenominational worship service in the center of town. There's no preaching, just praise and worship interspersed with testimonies and prayer. Last week the main part of the meeting had just finished and I was heading toward the kitchen to grab a pot of coffee when one of the women stopped me.

A wonderful woman I respect and adore, Norma Lee, took my hands and said, "I've been feeling like the Lord wants me to tell you something. He wants you to know that he desires to spend more time with you. And as you spend more time in his presence, just communing with him, there are things he will begin to share with you concerning the desires of your heart."

This isn't the first time someone has felt directed to say this kind of thing to me.

Once about ten years ago, a woman from my church phoned me at home. Gaynelle sounded slightly embarrassed as she said, "I don't usually do this, call people like this, but I haven't been able to shake the sense that I'm supposed to tell you something. God wants you to know that he's waiting for you in the garden. He wants to walk with you and talk with you. He's waiting for you. He wants you to join him there. He knows you're busy, but he misses you, and he's waiting for you in the garden. I'm sorry . . . I hope you don't think I'm crazy or anything. Does it make any sense? Does it mean anything to you?"

She didn't know I'd been struggling with some big challenges in my life and that, truth be told, I'd been avoiding God altogether for months.

I took a deep breath. "Actually, yeah. It makes a lot of sense. And, no, I don't think you're crazy. Your words *do* mean something to me. Very much so."

But here's the weird part. You'd think I would have felt dread, being summoned like that by the very One I'd been trying to avoid. Or maybe scolded just a little. Or at least embarrassed to have a message like that delivered to me via a third party. But I didn't feel any of those things.

Actually I felt relief. Something in her words resonated deep inside of me, and I knew that spending time with God in a quiet place was more than a nice idea, more than a timely suggestion, more than a prudent choice. It was, indeed, exactly what I needed, something I'd been longing for, and the very purpose for which I'd been created in the first place.

Wish you were here

Amazing stuff happens when we spend time in the presence of God. Sometimes we get answers to problems we've been whining about for months. Sometimes we get answers to questions we've never even asked. Sometimes we don't get any answers at all. Instead, we walk away filled with a delicious sense of satisfaction and completion.

And, every now and then, we get surprised.

Several years ago Kacie and I were driving to church. I think she was all of, I don't know, maybe eight at the time, and she was complaining about church being boring and asking why she even had to go.

I believe her exact words were, "It's boring. Why do I even have to go?"

I pursed my lips in thought. Finally, I said, "You know, Jesus is there. We're going to his house. And, like visiting with anyone at their house, we can have a conversation with him there. We can tell him things and he can tell us things too. So let's ask him for two things, okay? Let's ask him now, before we even get there."

Kacie looked dubious at best. "Yeah? Like what?"

"Let's ask him to help us sense that he's there, in the room with us. You know how when you're in a room by yourself and someone else walks in, sometimes you know they're there even before you see them or they make a sound? Like that. Second, let's ask him to share something with us while we're there, like a secret. Now maybe he will and maybe he won't. It's up to him and whatever he decides is fine with us, so we don't need to 'try' to make it happen. But we're going to ask him for these two things. Then it's up to him."

She shrugged her compliance, and we prayed together, saying "Amen" about the time I pulled the car into the church parking lot.

Fifteen minutes later, during the praise and worship portion of the service, I glanced at my daughter standing next to me. Kacie was looking down at the floor so I could only see the top of her head. What was she doing? Sleep-standing? Counting carpet strands? Obviously she was as bored as she'd predicted she would be. I shrugged and thought, *Oh well, at least I tried*, and refocused my attentions on God.

Later, driving home, I casually asked what she'd thought of the service.

When she spoke, her voice contained an unexpected blend of embarrassment and awe. She said, "When we were singing, I started crying and I couldn't stop. So I put my head down so no one would see, but I couldn't stop crying."

I glanced quickly at her, surprised. "What kind of feeling were you having? Sad? Happy? Frustrated? Bored? A feeling you can't put into words? Disappointed? Annoy—"

She lit up. "Wait! Stop! That one—a feeling you can't put into words!"

I know that feeling. I said, "Kacie, that was the Holy Spirit. You were feeling God's presence."

She nodded as if I hadn't told her anything she hadn't already known. She went on, "By the time the singing was over, I'd stopped crying, but during the entire sermon I felt like I was going to start again any minute. And I don't know if this is a secret or not, but when the pastor was talking, I realized something I'd never thought about before. For the first time, I really understood how much God loved me, and that there's nothing I can do to make that love go away or get smaller."

It was my turn to nod. When I could, I swallowed past the lump in my throat and said, "Wow! He answered your prayer, Kacie. He really answered your prayer."

Here's what I *didn't* tell her: When I'd suggested we pray that morning, I'd done it for Kacie. I wasn't expecting anything for me. I'd simply wanted Kacie to experience God in a fresh way.

During praise and worship, I did what I usually try to do, which is spend that time really thinking about the One I'm singing to—not about me, not about my problems, but about God. As I sang, I pictured him sitting on an elevated golden throne, all majestic and holy and regal. The Bible calls him King of Kings and Lord of Lords, and I pictured him just like that, then imagined myself standing off at a distance, in a courtyard below his throne, worshiping him. He was, after all, the King, the Almighty God, the Creator of the Universe, the Judge and Savior of the World, the Great I Am.

All of a sudden, something happened in the little scenario I was creating and enjoying, except I didn't plan it or imagine it. It took me completely by surprise, and I simply watched in amazement as this scene unfolded before my eyes. God stood up. Descending a small flight of steps, he walked to me. Then the Holy One, the King of Kings, the Almighty God, gazed into my eyes, opened his arms, and said tenderly, "Dance with me."

My eyes flew open. I blinked several times, trying to absorb what I'd just experienced. On stage, musicians sang and played; around me people sang and praised. How could everything around me seem so normal and yet transformed at the very same time?

Dance with me . . .

What a surprise! The picture I'd been crafting in my head was of an eternal, omnipotent, holy God worthy of worship from afar. And yet there he was, standing before me as a lover, arms open, inviting me to dance, eternal, omnipotent, and holy but also attentive and present and intimate. *This* was the picture he wanted me to have of him. I smiled and whispered, "Yes, I *will* dance with you."

Then I closed my eyes again and stepped into his embrace.

Breathe, just breathe

I remember, as a little girl, the scent of my mother's breath as she kissed me.

I remember drinking in the fragrance of the milky sweet breath of my newborn babies.

I remember being with someone I loved and the warmth of his breath on the curve of my skin between my neck and my shoulder. I remember slow dancing in my kitchen and the way his breath felt on my cheek. I remember the sound of his breathing while he slept.

I think there is no music more intimate than the sound of the flute. I have always been enchanted by the intimacy of the sound of the drawn breaths of the flutist as she plays.

My guess is that you've had similar experiences. In so many contexts breath and intimacy go hand in hand. But breath isn't just associated with *intimacy*, it's also associated with *life*. After all, God breathed into the nostrils of an inanimate Adam, bringing him to life. You and I breathe to live.

Breathing is also vital to emotional and physical *health*. When we're on the verge of panic, there's a good chance someone will remind us to *breathe, just breathe* and in doing so, sometimes we find a way to reconnect with equilibrium and hope and strength. Athletes and others use hyperbaric oxygen chambers to get more oxygen into their bodies with every breath, allowing their bodies to heal faster from wounds and injuries. Breathing coach Michael White teaches people new breathing patterns to maximize their intake of oxygen. The health benefits include less stress, better skin tone, deeper sleep, weight loss, and reduced odds for life-threatening diseases such as cancer.

Intimacy. Life. Health.

There's another breath that gives us all these things and more, and it's the breath of God.

The Bible was originally written in Hebrew and Greek, and in these languages the words used for "Spirit" are *current* or *wind* or *breath*. In other words, the Holy Spirit is the breath of God.

We need breath.

We need the life it imparts.

We need the health it enables.

We need the intimacy it brings.

And to thrive—*really* thrive—we need to spend time in the presence of God, drawing so near to him we can close our eyes and feel his very breath.

It's easy to lose our sense of happiness, peace, and hope when our circumstances go awry. It's even easier when, in addition to everything else, we're not taking care of our most basic needs.

So get a good night's sleep. Get plenty of exercise. Eat right and drink lots of water. Consume large amounts of chocolate, and make frivolous purchases of new shoes whenever you can.

And above all, don't forget to breathe.

Turn on a Light

- What does breath symbolize for you?

- When you think of intimacy, life, and health, is there one that stands out more than the rest as something you long to experience more fully in your life?

- The breath of God seems pretty personal and intimate, not something we would necessarily associate with a distant, angry God, an intangible Life Force, the Big Guy Upstairs, or with the idea that God is everywhere and everything. Regardless of what you've heard or believe, don't you *wish* it could be true? Don't you long for someone in your life who is not only eternal, all-knowing, all-powerful, and all-good, but who actually *knows* you and *loves* you?

  If someone like this actually existed, what would you say to him? My guess is that it might go something like this: "I've always wanted a relationship with someone like you, but I'm scared. I'm still not sure you exist the way I want you to exist, and I don't want to be disappointed. And, too, I hear so many conflicting opinions about who you are and what you're like, so that's also scary.

  "But maybe it's time to stop going on hearsay. What if you're for real and I never gave you a chance? Maybe it's time to find out for myself.

"All I know is that deep inside, I long for intimacy, life, and health, and I've been told that the desire of your heart is to give me all of these things through the death and resurrection of your Son Jesus. You're not just saying, 'Believe in me,' you're saying, 'Dance with me.' That's what I want too. So here I am. Here's my heart. I want something personal and intimate, something life-giving and real. Do I want you in my life? Do I dare believe? Will I dance with you? My answer to all is yes."

11

Follow Your Dreams (Except the One Where You're at School in Your Underwear)

The other day Kacie hollered excitedly from the kitchen, "Hey, Mom! Wanna see something cool?"

I walked into the kitchen. She was perched on a stool, leaning over the counter, staring into a cup of tea with ecstasy on her face. She said, "Watch this." She lifted the teabag by its string and dangled it above the cup. Then she blew on an edge of the teabag and watched it spin. "Isn't that amazing?"

My kids are passionate about the weirdest stuff.

Kaitlyn's bookshelves are filled with books on apologetics. Now these aren't books I've purchased for her or books she's been forced to read by machine-gun-toting militia. This is stuff she buys and reads on her own. You know, for fun.

I don't get it. When I was her age, I was reading Phyllis Whitney, which is kinda like Nancy Drew for older girls because the heroine usually gets to fall in love at some point during the adventure. So Kaitlyn's passion is beyond me. Not that I'm not supportive, I am. One year for her birthday the only thing she wanted was the 150-dollar registration fee to attend a conference on this very subject. So I gave it to her. Why not? It seems like a worthy enough endeavor, although I'm not sure how seriously she takes all this stuff. One day I asked her how she can read all those books on apologetics and *still* have a hard time saying she's sorry after a fight. She just laughed at me, which didn't seem like much of an answer, but it was nice to see she could handle a little constructive criticism without losing her sense of humor.

As for me, well . . . I'm passionate about a lot of stuff, but lately I've been particularly enamored with craigslist .org. It's this huge online garage sale. I click on the name of my city and suddenly I have access to a cornucopia of secondhand treasures! Among my acquisitions so far have been two love seats, a metal bench, five ceiling fans, various houseplants, a set of dishes, a huge mirror for my living room, and Jieils.

No, I didn't find Jieils in "furniture." I found him in "professional services." He has a flooring business, and I hired him to pull out some ugly plaid basement carpet and replace it with all those twenty boxes of laminate I bought at the Home Depot. Several odd jobs later (and

I do mean "odd"—one of his assignments was to help build a sea cave in Kacie's underwater-themed room) we've sort of adopted him into the family. I think my sister Renee thought of it first. Her exact words were "Let's adopt Jieils."

See why craigslist.org is so much fun? Where else can you find furniture, light fixtures, and even friends?

My kids are putting pressure on me to slow it down. They think I have some sort of addiction. They've already put me on craigslist restriction and are threatening an inpatient treatment program if I don't get a grip.

The good news is that I think I know how to win them over. All I have to do is get them as hooked on this website as I am. I'll start with Kacie. She's young enough that I still harbor the illusion that I can outsmart her. The next time I'm on craigslist I'll search for something that'll make Kacie do a double take. I'm thinking teabag wind chimes might do the trick.

Passionate about our problems

I can also feel passionate about my troubles. Whenever circumstances are askew in my life, those circumstances—and how I feel about them—can consume me for hours, months, or years.

Some time ago my husband and I attended a Christmas concert featuring Sandi Patty. Since Larry had gone to college with Sandi, we were invited backstage after the event. While waiting for Sandi to join us, we introduced ourselves to another backstage guest who turned out to be the drummer in a seventies band my husband had listened to for years.

When my husband asked Tom what he'd been doing since the band's breakup in '76, Tom said, "I partied in the seventies. In the eighties I struggled a lot with depression. The nineties were recovery years."

I was fascinated by the way he took a single category of circumstances and used it to define an entire decade. Ten whole years had been summed up by the word *parties*. *Depression* had a decade to itself, as did *recovery*.

Tom was obviously a big-picture kind of guy. I can relate. I do the same thing, which is to let a single circumstance or a single emotion monopolize my life for, like, a *really* long time. During that period of time—whether it's a day or a decade—the circumstance seems to set the tone for my entire life. It consumes my focus, preoccupies my attention. My energies are completely devoted to pondering my problem, wrestling with angst over my problem, complaining about my problem, obsessing about my problem, despairing over my problem.

Even when my problem renders me dispassionate, inert, and exhausted, I am *wholeheartedly* engrossed in my dispassion, inertia, and exhaustion, which, if you ask me, is a kind of passion after all.

You know exactly what I'm talking about, don't you? I have no doubt there've been times in your life when unpleasant circumstances have completely occupied your every thought. Who knows? You might be feeling that way right now. It could be the very reason you started reading this book in the first place.

And, sure, you could tell yourself to simply stop thinking about it, but we all know how *that* works, right? All I have to do is say, "Whatever you do, *don't* think about penguins," and images of those tuxedoed bipeds will be stuck in your head as stubbornly as the lyrics to some radio jingle you've heard one too many times and can't shake for days.

What's worse, even if you *do* succeed at forgetting about your painful circumstance for a few heartbeats, what happens? More often than not, something comes along to refresh your memory.

One day, while traveling to and from Denver, I drove past the freeway exit that would have taken me to Skippy's house, which was *definitely* not my destination. Nevertheless, all day long I endured memories I couldn't seem to shake no matter how hard I tried. And I really did try. Eventually I succeeded at what I hadn't been able to do for hours and managed to banish all unwanted thoughts. Whew! Finally! What a relief! It was great. I hadn't thought about Skippy at *all* for maybe fifteen minutes when I decided to return a few phone calls. One number I needed was in a saved voice message, so I called my voice mail. After listening to several messages, I got to the one I wanted, wrote down the phone number, and deleted the message. Before I could hang up, I heard an automated voice say, "Message deleted. Next saved message . . ." and then his voice.

Great. Just *great*.

Unfortunately, reminders can come in many forms. Unrelated things can remind us of whatever we're trying to forget. Do you remember the song "King of Pain" by the Police? The song is about someone who's in a world of hurt and, as a result, everything he sees—a black hat caught in a tree, a dead salmon frozen in a waterfall, a flag reduced to shreds by a merciless wind—manages to take on a darker meaning and remind him of the pitiful situation he's in.

Passionate about your pain? Exchange that passion for a new one!

Sometimes life hands us stuff we can't control. That stuff can evoke intense emotions we don't want, don't enjoy, can't seem to put down, and, sometimes, have a hard time escaping, though we really do try!

I wish we could take care of these emotions the same way I took care of the curtains I bought a few weeks ago. When I got them home and realized they weren't the color I wanted after all, I took 'em right back, handed them to the clerk at the returns counter and—ta da!— they were out of my life forever.

Unfortunately, a different return policy can apply to emotions. For example, most of the time when I try to take my angst to the returns counter, the clerk merely shakes her head and points to the sign that says, "No Returns. Exchanges Only."

I used to argue with her, but it hardly ever worked, so I've been adjusting. I've even complied with the exchange policy a few times, and I have to admit that this annoying policy actually has merit. Sometimes the best way to get rid of intense emotions really *is* to replace them with something better.

I'm not saying we can't have more than one passion. But passions, especially new passions, are ravenous creatures, consuming more than their fair share of our thoughts, time, and resources. We can't feed too many at once. This is why, when new passions show up on the scene, old passions are replaced or at least become "interests" rather than "passions."

We've heard for years that one way to get over a broken heart is to fall in love with someone else. But this doesn't just work with broken hearts. Truthfully, there are times when the best way to get over an emotional attachment to *any* unpleasant circumstance may be to attach our heart to something else that happens to be bigger and better, something wonderful, something that sets us to bubblin' with peace, happiness, or hope.

Got bubbles?

I was *definitely* not bubbling. Six months of depression had given way to another three or four months of, well, just feeling worn out and blue. It seemed as if I'd been hit hard on every front and I was emotionally exhausted.

This was my condition one afternoon last month when my oldest daughter plopped herself down on the bed where I was reading. She said, "I've been thinking."

I put down my book and smiled. "I'll alert the media."

"I know *exactly* what you need," she said confidently.

"Oh?"

"Sometimes we've gotta look past what's going on in our own world and reach out," she said passionately. "You know, serve others. What if you volunteered somewhere? How 'bout at church? You could work the coffee bar or start a small group. Or volunteer somewhere in the community. I don't know. Soup kitchen? Some sort of literacy program? It would take your mind off stuff and I think you'd feel better."

I felt tears well up behind my eyeballs. Holding them back and trying not to sound hurt or defensive, I said, "Kaitlyn, that's the *last* thing I need. Sometimes it feels as though I carry the world on my shoulders as it is! I definitely don't need *more* responsibility. I think I just need to take care of myself for a while."

Later, when she'd gone upstairs, I remembered her comment and thought, *Honestly! As if a majority of my life isn't spent taking care of people as it is! She thinks I need to serve more? That's the last thing I need!*

In the following weeks, the weirdest thing happened.

When my youngest daughter, Kacie, told me she didn't want to go to church summer camp because she didn't really know anyone in the youth group, I started thinking about all the junior high kids who feel the same way, and how truly hard it is—at any age—to go cold into a group and start making new friends. Two days later I called our youth pastor and offered to host a barbecue at my house for all the families with junior high students so our kids could hang out and get to know each other. Thrilled, Pastor Jordan said my timing couldn't have been better since the staff had *just* been brainstorming about how to generate greater community among the junior high kids!

The more I thought about everything, the more passionate I felt. I'd been thinking about joining a home Bible study, but suddenly what I wanted more than anything was to start a small group for families with kids in that amazing, unpredictable, precarious, hilarious stage of life between, say, eleven and fourteen.

When I told Kacie we were going to do that very thing, she rolled her eyes and groaned. "Mom! I can't believe you did that!" In her next breath, all the disdain in her voice gave way to a thin layer of caution covering bubbles of excitement as she blurted, "So will everyone get to come to our house?"

I was bubbling too.

That night I started painting the basement. Already equipped with a ping pong table, a couple couches, and a TV, it was the perfect adolescent hangout place. But it definitely needed some sprucing up.

So I went to craigslist.

That was a week ago, and since then I've purchased two floor lamps (10 dollars each), a red loveseat (125 dollars), and a wicker ottoman with a 300-dollar price tag still attached (I paid 50 dollars). In other words, I've pretty much remodeled my entire basement for less than 200 bucks.

Long live craigslist.org!

Camp starts in four days. Tonight we're having a Pre-Camp S'mores Fest. About a dozen kids are invited. And in a few weeks we'll have the BBQ Jordan and I discussed. And after that we'll see how many families would like to get together on a regular basis.

And you know what? I'm not feeling so worn out and blue anymore. Oh, I still have my days. But lately I've been having other kinds of days too, days when there's energy in my veins and vision in my brain. I haven't felt those things in a while, and it's cool, very cool.

Kaitlyn was right.

There was wisdom in what she'd said to me, but somehow I missed it the first time around. Maybe if I'd been listening—*truly* listening—I could have heard past what she was saying to, well . . . what she was saying.

She wasn't saying I needed more *responsibility* in my life. She was saying I needed more *passion* in my life, something I cared about (besides my woes), something that would spark a vision in me, something that would energize me, something that would get my brain tumbling and my creative juices flowing, something that would make me *bubble*.

What makes *you* bubble?

My dad teaches a monthly seminar on biblical and motivational principles. (It's been his passion for decades. Maybe it's true what they say about apples not falling too far from the tree.) In any case, not too long ago he asked me to come up with some sort of exercise that everyone could do at the beginning of one of his sessions.

The first thing I did was run by the market and pick up a giant can of fruit cocktail.

On the night of his presentation, I gave everyone a piece of paper and asked them to fold it in half and crease the fold really well. At the top of the paper, above the crease, I asked them to write down one or more things they'd always thought they would have done, become, experienced, or accomplished by now. At the bottom of the paper, below the crease, I asked them to write down whatever had kept them from doing, becoming, experiencing, or accomplishing that dream.

And then I gave the microphone back to my dad.

As always, he delivered an inspiring and practical message. In it, he showed everyone several ways they could take greater control of their lives and what the outcomes of their choices would be. After an inspiring hour, he waved me forward.

Back in front of the group, I lit a fire in the fruit cocktail can (I'd removed the fruit). Then I took my paper from earlier in the evening and ripped it apart at the seam. I took the bottom half—the one on which I'd written down whatever had kept me from doing, becoming, experiencing, or accomplishing my dreams, set it on fire, and dropped it in the can.

Kacie was the first one to join me.

My teenaged nephews Connor and Hunter were quick to follow suit, as were Kaitlyn and her friends, Jess, Kevin, Dan, and Brandie. I figured I could count on all these kids, but I thought the parade might end there.

I was wrong.

I won't swear that *everyone* there that night watched their limitations go up in smoke, but I'm pretty sure almost everyone did.

Norma Lee was there. I've mentioned her before. She's been married a long time, with kids and grandkids. I know she's seen a lot of her dreams come true. After the meeting ended, she passed me on the way to the cookie table. She said, "Well, so much for resting on my laurels and just sittin' around watching my grandkids grow!"

I didn't need to ask her if that was a good thing or a bad thing. The animation on her face and the lilt in her voice said it all. She was beaming. More than beaming, she was *bubblin'*.

As far as I can tell, some abandoned passion got rekindled for her that night. Someday I'll ask her to tell me what it was. Or maybe I won't need to ask. Maybe in the not-so-distant future I'll hear that Norma Lee has written a book, established an orphanage, run in the Boston Marathon, or moved to Italy. Anything's possible when you're passionate.

Why don't you try the list thing I just described? On one piece of paper, write down one or more things you've always wanted to do, become, experience, or accomplish. On a second piece of paper, write down whatever has held you back. Now throw *that* piece of paper away. Who knows? Maybe the thing that'll catch fire will be *you*.

I don't know about you, but I'm tired of feeling passionate about my problems. I'm more than ready to feel passionate about something grander than the hiccups (and even the hurricanes) in my own personal world. I'm ready to take my time, energy, thoughts, and resources and start feeding different purposes and priorities. I'm ready to feel passionate about my dreams.

I'd write more on this subject, but I've really gotta go. One of my passions is calling me. I'm going straight to craigslist.org. But this time I'm not shopping. Nosiree. This time I'm going to post an ad.

Surely there's *someone* out there looking to buy a ziplock bag filled with four pounds of fruit cocktail.

Turn on a Light

- What have you felt passionate about this week?

- When you think about pursuing something you've always wanted to become, do, or accomplish, do you think, *But I don't have the time or energy for that!* There's wisdom in not taking on too much and knowing when it's too soon to take on a new endeavor. And yet sometimes passions can energize us, giving us more oooomph and up-and-at-'em than we had before. What are signs that it might be the right time for you to fire up a new passion?

- What's holding you back? Take the quiz on www .businessknowhow.com/career/passion/quiz3.htm from the book *The Passion Plan: A Step-by-Step Guide to Discovering, Developing, and Living Your Passion* by Richard Chang (San Francisco: Jossey-Bass, 2000).

12

Where Are We Going and Why Am I in This Handbasket?*

My sister and I had just spent several hours hunting for treasures at Hobby Lobby. After a plunder-filled morning, we were loading our respective purchases in our respective cars when it dawned on me that my 4Runner was as lopsided as a peg-legged pirate marooned on an island infested with termites. I didn't *just* have a flat tire. That baby was squashed, annihilated, obliterated. The metal rim was resting on the ground and the rubber tire around it was as shapeless as pulp.

Luckily, one of the store clerks—a high school junior named Trevor—offered to change the tire for me.

I opened the hatchback of my 4Runner.

*A small basket, usually used in the phrase "to hell in a handbasket," meaning a rapid and utter ruination (*Webster's Collegiate Dictionary*).

I've already humiliated myself enough by describing the inside of my car in a previous chapter. Let me simply say that the back of my car was filled with so much junk that—even after unloading as much as we could into the back seat—we still couldn't get to the hidden compartment containing the jack and the doodad thingie we needed to lower the spare tire from its storage compartment under the car.

We tried a long time, though.

Eventually Trevor had to return to his own life (he was in his late twenties by now and finishing grad school), and my sister gave me a ride back to my house.

Renee and I returned the next morning with a new strategy and reinforcements on the way. After pulling a half dozen cardboard boxes and trash bags out of her Montero, we got to work emptying my car of its various and sundry residents. These included six cans of spray paint, wrapping paper and Scotch tape, canned goods that had fallen out of various grocery bags over the years, five winter coats, a metal shovel, three glass doorknobs, a box of carpet samples, and a bucket of gloves and weeding tools.

Jieils had agreed to come by around ten and change the tire for me. Shortly after he got there, he found the jack and the doodad thingie (turns out they weren't buried in the back of the truck after all but stowed neatly under the back seat) and got busy loosening lug nuts. In the meantime, Renee and I continued digging and sorting.

We were about halfway through when Renee said, "What's this?"

I looked up. "What's what?"

"This."

I squinted. "Looks like mail."

"I *know* that. My point is, none of it's addressed to you."

Sure enough, she was holding a stack of mail—all of it addressed to other people.

I didn't remember seeing it before. I often grab my mail from my curbside mailbox when I'm pulling out of my driveway, tossing everything on the floorboard until I get back home. Apparently the mailman had delivered a batch of letters to my house that didn't belong to me. They had ended up on my floorboard and stayed there.

We laughed about it, although I'm guessing that with the release of this book, El Paso County will issue a warrant for my arrest for tampering with U.S. mail.

Renee and I continued pulling oddball items out of my truck and sorting them into the appropriate box or trash bag. She held up a pair of pants. "Do you want these?"

I looked closely. "I've never seen them before in my life."

"First you have other people's mail in your car and now other people's *clothes*?"

Even Jieils, from somewhere under my car, started to laugh.

My eyes grew wide. "Ohmigosh! That explains everything! *That's* why it's always a mess! Hobos are *living* in my truck!"

I was still defending my hypothesis ten minutes later as Jieils, announcing that the tire was changed, started putting away the tools. Renee tied up the tops of the bags of trash then hefted them into her Montero for a trip to a trash bin. As I loaded the last box into my backseat I tried one more time to convince them. "No, really," I said. "I'm sure of it. That's what's going on."

No one seemed to believe me.

Renee agreed with me on one thing, though. Jieils did a great job changing that tire. I'm glad I called him. If he hadn't shown up, my 4Runner would probably *still* be sitting in that parking lot, which would be tragic.

Where would the hobos sleep then?

Crash, Dummy!

Unfortunately, some problems aren't as easily solved as a flat tire.

When my publisher and I came up with the idea for this book, I was thrilled. I told them, "I *totally* want to do this book. This is where I live. I've been living this stuff for the past several years. In fact I can write this book with one hand tied behind my back . . . as long as, of course, you don't mind a few typos."

The truth is, for the past couple years I've been careening nonstop ninety miles an hour through some pretty stressful terrain. How stressful? Well, let's see . . . I launched and sold a small business, relocated to a new city, invited several friends and family members to live with me during transitions in their lives, faced financial challenges, injured my foot and hobbled around in pain for months. Within my extended family there have been some challenges and heartache that have impacted me greatly. In unrelated circumstances, I lost two close friends. And when two people I love and admire admitted their marriage had gone into cardiac arrest, I spent countless hours grieving with them, nagging them into counseling, and basically doing anything else I could think of in a frantic effort to see this marriage healed.

Not to mention the whole Skippy thing.

So, yeah, it's been hard. Overall, I've struggled to stay on top of things. Particularly over the past eighteen months, my peace keeps going AWOL, my hope is on Prozac, and my happiness keeps waking up on the wrong side of the bed.

To deal with all this, I've been personally practicing every single one of the strategies I've written about in this book. I've been getting my body moving, walking and biking and even belly dancing. I've strived for healthier self-talk, mental images, and choices. I don't freak out when I have a temporary setback. I keep reminding myself that there are good things coming my way. I have faith in God and listen for his still, small voice.

And all these things have served me well. I can't imagine what kind of emotional state I'd be in this very moment if I *hadn't* been making a conscious effort to free my emotions from the tyranny of my circumstances. This is why I feel so passionate about sharing these strategies with you. I know firsthand the difference they can make.

Oh, and I added one other thing into the mix, and you'll need to remember to add it too. It's *time*. When it comes to rising above your circumstances, getting rogue emotions under control, or healing up after hurt or trauma, it can happen in a heartbeat or it can take months and even years. In these instances, patience is a virtue. Not lazy-like-a-pig-patience as in "There's nothing I can do so I guess I'll just wallow in this until it goes away on its own," but savvy-like-a-fox-patience. Savvy patience says, "While I'm waiting for time to do what *she* can do, I'll keep doing what *I* can do, which is actively manage my memories and my emotions in the healthiest way I know how." Savvy patience seeks and celebrates overnight success but doesn't freak out if healing and changes occur over months instead of minutes. Savvy patience says, "You're doing great. You've already come a long way. Now keep going and don't give up."

So I was doing all that.

Still . . .

A couple months ago something dawned on me. I told a friend, "I've made *huge* progress, but I'm still not where I'd like to be. I'm still struggling. For example, I'm still grieving losses that are a year old, isolating myself more than I'd like, sighing more than usual. Do you know what I think? I think I might be kinda stuck. Which means it's probably a good time to ask for help."

The last time I'd been stuck and needed a change, I'd picked up the phone and called Jieils. Unfortunately, this time it was going to take more than a tire jack and lug wrench to get me back up to speed.

I decided to call a few folks and see if anyone knew of a good counselor.

A few weeks passed. I kept meaning to make those phone calls.

In the meantime, the strangest thing happened. I hit a sudden lull in my life. Family left for vacation. Friends had other commitments. My kiddos were all gone visiting friends or on summer trips. Unrelated absences overlapped and, almost overnight, my life was void of distractions, people to take care of, emergencies to manage, and fires to put out. I took a deep breath and thought, *Great! I can spend this time writing*.

Guess what I did instead? I started crying and didn't stop for three whole weeks.

Everything in this book will make a difference in your life. I promise. But sometimes you'll do everything you know to do, and you'll keep doing it and do it some more, until you realize you're kinda stuck. You're not moving forward anymore. The scenery hasn't changed in a long time, and you realize you're experiencing *déjà glue*, which is the strange feeling you've been stuck here before.

Not that you stop making all the healthy choices I've been encouraging. You continue managing your memories and shaking your booty and muzzling your inner Eeyore. You still hang uplifting pictures on the walls of your mind rather than depressing, limiting images. You keep working on replacing fatalistic thinking with faith. You still feed your need for intimacy with God. And you're patient too. You don't get discouraged and give up just because you realize it's taking longer than the length of a sitcom to turn your life around.

Still . . .

Your wheels are spinning and you realize that to *really* get where you wanna be, you're probably going to need a good push.

So who ya gonna call?

Roadside assistance

Let me tell you what my neighbor Monica did when she found herself in this very place. She had just come through a dark tunnel filled with oncologists and fatigue and tests and treatments and decisions and talk of life and death and odds. The good news was that she had recently been told she was in remission and could pick up her old life where she had dropped it two years back. The bad news is that, instead of feeling relief, she felt more terrified than ever.

Monica explains, "While the cancer was active, at least there was something I could *do* about it. All the treatments and appointments gave me something to focus on, specific actions I could take. I felt a sense of control. But as soon as I was 'cured,' my spirits plummeted. I was still living with a threat of death—this kind of cancer often returns within two years—but now that treatments were unnecessary, there was nothing I could *do* to fight back. As a result, I felt more vulnerable and afraid than when I'd been sick."

Monica was preoccupied with her own mortality. She thought about it every day. Making any plans for the future seemed pointless. She became hyperaware of her own body, convinced that every ache or pain was signaling the beginning of the end.

For over a year Monica did everything she could think of to lift her spirits above her circumstances. She exercised. She gave herself pep talks. She sought advice and encouragement from friends. These things helped, and some days she really did feel a measure of peace and happiness and joy. But overall, Monica still felt fearful and hopeless much of the time. Eventually she heard about _____. She realized she wasn't "getting over it" on her own and decided to get some help.

My mom faced a different problem. She wasn't fearful or hopeless, she was *mad*. She'd been mad for more than a year.

Granted, her fury was justified. Something had happened in her life that would have raised the hackles of a professional saint. Card-carrying martyrs would have lashed back in anger. Even masochists with the words "Whip me, beat me, make me write bad checks" tattooed across their backs would have said, "Now *that* crosses the line."

In other words, she had a right to be angry.

But like the guy who drives blindly into an intersection because he's got the green light—and gets broadsided by the semitruck that just ran a red—just because you have a *right* to do something doesn't necessarily mean doing it will reward you with a long, happy life.

Sometimes, to get where we wanna be, we have to forfeit a few rights along the way. And if we can't do that on our own, we may have to ask for a little roadside assistance.

My mom remembers getting that assistance. "An international ministry was holding a one-day conference in my city," she told me. "The theme of the conference was freedom. I attended the conference and at the end of the evening, I asked one of the speakers to pray for me. I had lived with my anger for far too long and I knew I needed deliverance from that emotion. After we prayed together, all that anger left me. I felt at peace and free for the first time in eighteen months."

I know someone else who couldn't seem to get past feelings of anger. He wasn't angry at any particular person or incident, but he had an explosive temper that was creating havoc in his life and relationships. After punching a mailbox and breaking his hand, he said enough is enough and got himself into anger management counseling.

I met a woman who got tired of feeling afraid and vulnerable after a former boyfriend knocked her out with a blow to her head and left her for dead. When she realized she wasn't getting over her fears on her own, Pam signed up for self-defense courses. Today not only has she conquered her fears, she's created a new career for herself, teaching self-defense tactics to women.

And you know that couple I mentioned earlier, the ones with the marriage in cardiac arrest? They were stuck too. She says, "We went through a similar crisis five years ago. We stayed together—barely—but it was more of a Band-Aid approach. We didn't know how to *really* fix anything and didn't turn to anyone else— counselors, pastors, marriage books, or seminars—who might have helped us figure it out. After five more years of suffering, we're once again in crisis and at the cross-roads of divorce. Part of me thinks, *We couldn't fix it last time, so let's just call it quits.* But another part of me says, *Sure, you couldn't fix it last time . . . but you also tried to fix it on your own. This time around, what if you got some help? Could it make a difference? Isn't it worth a try?"*

Right now this couple is rallying whatever roadside assistance they can think of: prayer intercessors, individual counselors, a marriage counselor, and relationship books and tapes. They may even pull a financial counselor into the mix before it's all said and done. Can this marriage be saved? I think it can. But whatever happens, this marriage deserves the chance to benefit from the insights that wise counselors and professionals can bring to the table.

Celebrating freedom

Where did I find help? Shortly after realizing I was stuck, determining to find a counselor, and then crying for three weeks, I got the push I needed.

It was the Sunday morning before Memorial Day and I'd gone to church. Instead of opening the service with our usual praise and worship, several folks read excerpts of letters from soldiers. It was a cool time of celebrating the freedom we enjoy as a nation and expressing gratitude to people who have sacrificed to make it happen. From there we segued into familiar worship songs. We started singing a song I've sung a thousand times. Okay, at least a hundred. It goes, "Lord, I give you my heart, I give you my soul . . ."

Suddenly a lightbulb went on in my head, except it was a brighter light than that, more like a spotlight or maybe even an atom bomb. For months I'd been asking myself why I was still grieving the whole Skippy thing. But as I sang those words—words I've sung before, mind you, without a single burst of bulb or bomb—a flash of clarity hit me between the eyes like a two-by-four (pardon the mixed metaphors but I'm on a roll here and in a hurry to get to the rest of the story). And for the first time in a year, I had my answer. Boy, oh boy, did I have my answer.

No wonder my heart was so stuck! When it came to heart and soul, I couldn't do much of anything because I'd given it all away to someone else. I'd even said those exact words: "I belong to you, heart and soul." Sappy, I know. And of course I hadn't given my *soul* soul, as in some sort of weird Nicolas Cage/*Ghost Rider* scenario. My *soul* soul belonged to Jesus, just as it had ever since I was a kid and told him he could have it.

But my point is that I'd *really* given this person my heart. And even though he'd been out of my life now for more than a year, I had never taken it back. What's more, I wasn't sure I could.

Not without help.

People around me were still singing, but not me. Suddenly I was praying with a fire and fervency unlike anything I've experienced in a very long time. The words came fast and furious, borne on the wings of some sort of heartfelt conviction that hadn't been there just thirty seconds before. I whispered urgently, "Lord, help me take my heart back. I want it back. Now. Today. *Today* is my day for freedom. Not tomorrow, not next week. Today. And you're the only one who can do it. I *do* give you my heart and soul, because we're taking it back together, you and me. It's yours. It's over. I'm free."

Something had happened. I knew it. But I wanted to make sure. I was done hurting. I wanted my freedom, and I wanted it *that* day, and nothing less would do. I wanted to ask another woman to pray with me, for me. Right then.

The minute the service ended, I went looking for Kim, our pastor's wife. I've been attending Rock Family Church for more than a year, and pretty much every Sunday that I'm there, Kim and I cross paths in the foyer and chat for several minutes. It's a small foyer. She's a friendly person. It's not rocket science.

I hung around for fifteen minutes. I'd spotted Kim in the service, but now she was nowhere to be found.

Driving home, I thought about phoning Kim and asking to meet her for coffee later in the week so we could pray together. I believe something wonderful and powerful happens when people pray together, and for the first time in a year, I was ready to enlist the help of anyone who could help me do what I needed to do, which was finish freeing my emotions from the boney grasp of painful circumstances.

The next day was Memorial Day, so I didn't call her then. The day after that I was busy doing stuff with my kids, so I didn't call her then. The next day I had a good day writing and puttering around the house, so I didn't call then either. That was almost a month ago.

I think it would have been great if Kim and I had prayed together. And who knows? If next week I feel some sort of a relapse coming on, she'll be the first person I call. But the truth of the matter is that something *did* happen that Sunday. When I got to the place where I was willing to do *whatever* I had to do—seek counseling, seek prayer, seek God—something happened. I passed a milestone in my journey to free my emotions from the tyranny of a particularly painful set of circumstances. In fact forget milestone. This was way bigger than a milestone. This was more like a bridge—the Golden Gate Bridge. And I crossed it and I'm not going back.

Glue-B-Gone

I went online and looked up ways to dissolve glue. I found remedies ranging from vegetable oil and lighter fluid to detergents and even perfume. But whatever you do, use something—Crisco, Cheer, or Coco Chanel. Don't stay stuck. Dissolve something, change something, pray something, or call someone, but don't give up, settle in, or resign yourself to a place of immobility forever.

In their book *What Happy Women Know*, Dan Baker and Cathy Greenberg write, "Happy people know that grief in itself is not a trap. Believing that you can never transcend it is."[4] The same goes for other emotions you might be mired in. Feeling bitter, angry, depressed, hopeless, powerless, or inferior doesn't determine your future. What determines your future is believing that you'll *always* be there.

"When you're going through hell, keep going." Winston Churchill said that, and it sure makes sense to me.

Things *can* change. They can change for the better and sometimes they even change for good. And if you're *really* stuck and in need of a change, call me. I'll send Jieils right over.

Turn on a Light

- What kinds of things tend to get you stuck?

- If you've been stuck before, what helped you get unstuck? And if you're stuck now, what would help you get moving again? Is there something you need to accept, forget, forgive, reframe, give up, identify, grieve, change, or ask for?

- Do you believe you can get unstuck?

- What roadside assistance have you used or could you call now if needed?

13

What Would Scooby Do?

We *know* what Scooby would do. Scooby would want a Scooby snack.

I think the more important question is this: What would *MacGyver* do? I mean, besides look gorgeous. If you're too young to remember the show, look it up online. M-a-c-G-y-v-e-r. You can see his picture on a number of sites. Yes, I know he looks really eighties. But it *was* the eighties, so go with it.

Richard Dean Anderson created the character of Angus MacGyver (yes, *Angus*), a resourceful secret agent with great hair, not to mention this uncanny knack for using common household items to get himself out of life-threatening dilemmas. Usually this was the highlight of the show. We got to watch MacGyver survive situations like getting trapped in a room with a ticking bomb and nothing on hand to save himself except, oh, I don't know, some dryer lint and a Bic pen.

Okay, I made up the part about the dryer lint. But the real story lines didn't sound any more plausible (although the fun of the show was that MacGyver's inventions were based on scientific principles and were technically possible even if they weren't all that probable).

For example, in one episode he had to destroy a laser. Thank goodness he had cigarettes and binoculars on hand!

He plugged a sulfuric acid leak with chocolate. He repaired a blown fuse using the aluminum wrapper of a stick of gum. He smashed through a door (and took out two armed guards) using a slingshot made from bedsprings.

He built a bomb from a fire extinguisher. He recharged a battery with wine. He fixed a broken fuel line with a ballpoint pen.

He blew open a truck door with a bomb he crafted out of pantyhose, an exhaust pipe, and an old battery. And when his getaway car had a broken radiator, all he could find to save himself were egg whites but—wouldn't you know it?—that was exactly what he needed to do the job. (Too bad *my* mechanic doesn't repair radiators with meringue! How can you go wrong with a repair technique that's so easy on the wallet, the environment, *and* the digestive tract?)

But hold on a second. Something just dawned on me. Now that I'm actually thinking about it . . . MacGyver had more to work with than mere egg whites. He had something going for him besides batteries and pantyhose, ballpoint pens, chewing gum, or chocolate. The thing MacGyver *really* had going for him was the belief that someway, somehow, he had access to whatever he needed to get himself out of the fix he was in.

I *think* I can. I **think** I can. I *think* I can.

Belief is a powerful thing. Henry Ford said, "Whether you think you can or think you can't, you're right." Even the Little Engine That Could learned that believing precedes succeeding. And while I may not be as savvy as the father of the entire auto industry, I figure I'm at *least* as smart as a cartoon train. So if the Little Engine was able to learn this lesson, so can I. And if *I* can learn it, you're the smart one, so it should be a piece of cake for you! (Or at least a slice of pie with meringue on top.)

If you and I are going to be survivors—and thrivers— we've gotta stop looking around at our seemingly hopeless circumstances, throwing up our hands, and throwing in the towel. Like MacGyver, we've got to adopt the attitude that we will *definitely* get through this. All we have to figure out is *how*.

What exactly did MacGyver do?

He stayed positive, always believing there was a way out of whatever mess he was in, and that he would soon figure out what it was.

He refused to be limited by his surroundings or his circumstances.

He loved learning and equipped himself ahead of time with knowledge he could use to get back on his feet the next time a crisis struck.

He wasn't a lone ranger but relied on friends and colleagues when he needed a helping hand.

He took whatever was in his life at the moment and put it to good use.

Have I mentioned he had great hair?

Finally, he kept his spirits high and stayed confident that—no matter how bad things looked—he had what it took to make it through.

You've got what it takes

You're probably thinking it was no big deal for Mac-Gyver to stay confident. After all, he had scriptwriters, the power of make-believe, *and* Henry "The Fonz" Winkler as the executive producer of his show.

On the other hand, what do *you* have? You might be surprised.

In addition to all your life experiences, education, common sense, and hard-won wisdom, you've acquired or sharpened about a dozen really great skills just by reading this book.

I've put together a list of things that—if you take to heart everything you and I have been talking about—you now have working on your behalf. Are you ready to hear what you know? Do us both a favor and read this list aloud:

I know that it's possible to experience peace, joy, and hope independent of my circumstances. (Chapter 1)

I know how to manage old and new memories. (Chapter 2)

I know how to tap into endorphins, adrenaline, and attitude. (Chapter 3)

I know how to choose the tone and content of my inner dialogue. (Chapter 4)

I know how to hang on to images that heal and empower. (Chapter 5)

I know how to take it in stride when I have a temporary setback. (Chapter 6)

I know how to choose life, making healthy choices whenever possible. (Chapter 7)

I know that good stuff exists outside the periphery of what I see and feel. (Chapter 8)

I know how to be still and listen. (Chapter 9)

I know how to take care of my basic needs, including my need for intimacy with God. (Chapter 10)

I know how to be inspired by big dreams. (Chapter 11)

I know how to get unstuck. (Chapter 12)

I know I'm gonna make it. (Chapter 13)

You and I will never have perfect lives. We'll never be surrounded by flawless circumstances. We'll probably never even have perfect hair. But here are thirteen things we *can* do. We are not without control. We've got more than we realize. We've got what we need. And we've *definitely* got what it takes.

All things work for good

It's easy to let our circumstances drag us under, but when we teach ourselves to *rise above* our circumstances— doing what is needed to live happy, fabulous lives even when our circumstances look dim—something really amazing can happen. Our circumstances don't just go from being negative to neutral, from detrimental to invisible, although that by itself would be a great thing, don't you think?

Instead, something even more miraculous can occur.

Our circumstances—even the yucky ones—can actually begin to *enrich* our lives. They can go from negative, *past* neutral and all the way to *positive*, from detrimental all the way to *beautiful*. What starts out looking like a liability can actually turn out to be an asset. The scuffs and scratches we thought would leave us ruined can become the very things that make us—like the Velveteen Rabbit—finally real. Problems that once incited groaning can start inspiring growth, and the circumstances that threatened to hold us back can be used as sails to propel us forward.

My dad does this thing sometimes. He hulks up, puts a scowl on his face, and growls, "I love problems! I eat 'em for breakfast! They give me *energy*!"

I wanna do that (except the scowl. I don't scowl, well . . . you know, at least not since the Botox).

My point is, wouldn't that be a great way to live? And I think we can get there, but only as we make choices every day to help us rise above the stuff going on in our lives.

I don't know about you, but I want to live above—not under—the rocks in my life. I want to stop letting painful stuff in my life smash me down or hold me under, and start letting it take me forward. After all, the same slab of granite can be a millstone, tombstone, or a stepping-stone. It can crush, signal the end, or create a path.

I'm voting for a path.

I'm not saying I have it all figured out, because I don't. I'm still learning how to use my problems as stepping-stones, still trying to grasp the idea that no experience in my life—no matter how bad—has to go to waste. Recently I almost let something go to waste, something big, something having to do with this very book.

I'm part of a writers' group. Rebecca Currington, founder of the Snapdragon Editorial Group, got us together last year, thinking that people who make a living writing and editing might have something in common besides weird facial tics and monthly therapy bills.

Turns out we really liked each other and have been getting together ever since. It's a small group but we're really committed. We meet every six weeks at my house and swap industry gossip, marketing strategies, proposal tips, agent recommendations, time management techniques, and even cash-flow-horror-stories (full-time writers always have *lots* of cash-flow-horror-stories!).

And in the process, we've grown from professional acquaintances to colleagues to friends. (Would anything less than a cadre of friends have gotten to see Mike Klassen's jar of belly button lint, which he has personally harvested from his very own navel on a weekly basis since he was sixteen?)

We met again last week, with most of the usual suspects—including Mike, Beth Leuders, Laura Lisle, and Andy Sloan—present and accounted for. We were still catching our breath from the news that Beth, assisted by Laura, had just completed her book *Lifting Our Eyes: Finding God's Grace through the Virginia Tech Tragedy*, when Mike turned to me and said, "So what's going on with *your* book? It's all turned in now, right?"

"Actually, no."

(Gasps all around the table.)

Then they all started asking questions at once. Wasn't it due last month? Was my publisher still speaking to me? How much more did I need to write? If I hadn't been finishing the book, what in the world *had* I been doing since the last time we'd all gotten together?

What had I been doing? Actually that was easy to answer. I told them briefly about my three-week crying jag, concluding by saying, "I think everything just caught up with me. Several years' worth of, I don't know, stuff. Hard stuff. Heartbreak. Stress. Stuff like that. The good news is that I'm okay now. I'm moving on. The bad news is that, with all that going on, I wasn't working at all on my book. But I'm going to start working again this week."

Someone asked, "You're going to put that in your book, right? About the crying?"

I blinked. "Well, actually, no. I mean, I hadn't thought about it. I didn't think it related . . ."

And to tell the truth, part of me was horrified at the suggestion. After all, sometimes I think I tell *way* too much about my personal foibles as it is. That thought was short-lived, however, because by then my brain had started to spin, making connections, seeing things I hadn't seen before.

Mike said, "You thought those weeks kept you from working. I think you *were* working. Sure, you weren't *writing* your last chapters, but you were still working hard. You were *living* them."

Laura and Andy agreed. My mind was still trying to grasp what everyone was saying. By then it was time to go. As everyone stood, stretched, grabbed notebooks and jackets, Beth said something very matter-of-factly, as if it summarized everything, as if it were the most obvious thing in the world.

She said, "Karen, you did it. You're done. You've finished the book. Now all you have to do is write it down."

When I started this book, I was in a dim place—not pitch-black but dim. And even though, like MacGyver, I knew that at some point before the credits rolled I'd be back to my old self, it sure didn't feel very good at the time.

I've practiced everything I've preached, and maybe I should do like those body makeover books and post before and after pictures. Except this book is about a makeover in the joy/peace/hope department, and my pictures would have to look something like this:

: (　　　　　　　: D

Before　　　　*After*

My point is, I did it and you can too.

Looking for peace, joy, and hope in all the wrong places

I have one last thing to say, and it's this. Peace, joy, and hope don't reside in our circumstances. If they did, every millionaire, every royal, and every celebrity—anyone at all residing in beautiful surroundings with access to plenty of money, opportunities, and adoration—would be ecstatic. But they aren't.

No. Joy, peace, and hope aren't in our circumstances. Oh, sometimes we see them there, but I think it's because our circumstances are like mirrors, or maybe the glassy surface of still waters, and sometimes it's possible to look at the surface of the things around us and see peace, joy, and hope reflected there.

But at other times our circumstances are clouded and murky, and no matter how we squint and strain, we can't see anything worth writing home about. But like a child who sees the moon in a puddle, stirs up the puddle with a stick, then looks into the muddy water and thinks the moon itself has been lost, is it possible that we're confusing reflection with the real thing?

Mud is real. Stress is real. Pain is real. Loss is real. And—stirred up in our lives—they can *definitely* obscure our peace, joy, and hope. But as long as our peace, joy, and hope don't *live* in our circumstances (and we could *attempt* to keep them there but, like relegating the moon to a puddle, why would we even want to try?), we've lost only the shine and not the substance.

So where *do* peace and happiness and hope reside? Wherever the storms can't reach. In ourselves; in our faith; in the never-changing nature of God; in the healthy choices we make; in our ability to love and, if we lose someone we've loved, to love again and again and again; in the healing quality of time; and in the resilience of the human spirit. And in the belief that we're going to make it after all.

Sometimes the tunnel is dark. Our surroundings are scary. Our circumstances are murky and opaque. But keep your hand on your purse and get ready to take action, baby! You're going to need your sunglasses sooner than you think.

Turn on a Light

- Did you ever watch MacGyver? Don't you agree he had great hair?

- If someone you loved asked your advice on how they could stop being crushed by a millstone in their life and, instead, turn it into a *milestone*, what would you tell them? Name three things.

- Have you ever heard of the MacGyver creed? Well, now you have. Repeat after me (and no cheating—it only counts if you say it out loud):

  Like MacGyver . . . I'm going to stay positive, always believing there's a way out of whatever mess I'm in and that I'll soon figure out what it is.

  I refuse to be limited by my surroundings or my circumstances.

  I'm going to keep learning, equipping myself ahead of time with knowledge I can use to get back on my feet the next time a crisis strikes.

  I'm not a lone ranger and I know how to receive encouragement, direction, and help from others.

  I have the ability to take whatever is in my life at this moment and put it to good use.

  I will keep my spirits high and stay confident that—no matter how bad things look—I really *do* have access to whatever it takes to make it through.

- How are you different after reading this book?

Notes

1. © 1998 by Pat Murphy. Go to www.exo.net/jaxxx/memory.
html. Originally published as an article in the *Magazine of Fantasy and Science Fiction*.

2. Emily Pronin and Daniel M. Wegner, "Manic Thinking: Independent Effects of Thought Speed and Thought Content on Mood," *Psychological Science* 17, no. 9 [2006]: 807–13.

3. A. A. Milne and Ernest H. Shepard, *Winnie the Pooh*, 80th Anniversary Edition (New York: Dutton, 2006), 65.

4. Dan Baker and Cathy Greenberg, *What Happy Women Know: How New Findings in Positive Psychology Can Change Women's Lives for the Better* (Emmaus, PA: Rodale, 2007), 155.

Karen Scalf Linamen is a motivational and inspirational speaker and the author of nine humorous self-help books for women. Her titles include *Just Hand Over the Chocolate and No One Will Get Hurt* and *Chocolatherapy: Satisfying the Deepest Cravings of Your Inner Chick*. She lives with her family in Colorado Springs, Colorado. Visit her at www.karenlinamen.com.